MOLLY BRANT

A Legacy of Her Own

by

Lois M. Huey and Bonnie Pulis

Old Fort Niagara Association, Inc.
Youngstown, New York
©1997
ISBN: 0-941967-18-2

OLD FORT NIAGARA PUBLICATIONS

Old Fort Niagara Association, Inc.
Fort Niagara State Park
P.O. Box 169
Youngstown, New York 14174-0169

Molly Brant: A Legacy of Her Own
is a production of the
Old Fort Niagara Association Publications program.

© Old Fort Niagara Association, Inc. 1997
    All rights reserved.
Fort Niagara State Park
Youngstown, New York

First Edition

ISBN: 0-941967-18-2
Printed on acid-free paper, in the United States of America.

Cover Illustrations:
Center: Portion of Molly Brant stamp; issued on April 14, 1986, by Canada Post
Corporation; Sara Tyson, artist. *Courtesy, Canada Post Corporation.*
Left: Sir William Johnson, by John Wollaston, c. 1751. *Courtesy, Albany Institute of
History & Art.*
Right: Joseph Brant, by Charles Willson Peale, c. 1797. *Courtesy, Independence
National Historical Park, Philadelphia, Pennsylvania.*

MOLLY BRANT

A Legacy of Her Own

To
Dr. Paul R. Huey
and
Wanda E. Burch

... for all their help and encouragement.

Table of Contents

Page

...continued...

Page

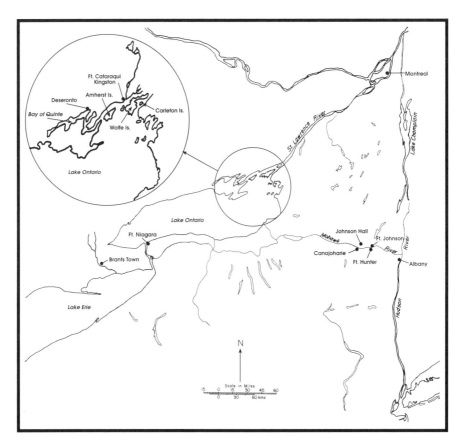

Primary sites in New York and Canada relative to Molly Brant.
Map by D.S. Knight.

**Judge Thomas Jones,
Chief Justice
of the
Supreme Court
for the
Colony of
New York.**

**Anne De Lancey Jones,
wife of
Judge Thomas Jones.**

Judge Jones wrote of visits to Sir William Johnson and Molly Brant, offering insight into Brant's personality and character. Following the American Revolution, Jones and his wife were named in the New York Act of Attainder and forbidden to return to the United States, under pain of death, because of their support for the Loyalist cause. Engravings by Charles Burt, after original paintings by R. Arnold (1791). From Edward Floyd De Lancey's (ed.) *History of New York During the Revolutionary War...by Thomas Jones,* **published in 1879, by the New-York Historical Society.**

Introduction
MOLLY BRANT

"Handsome, sensible, judicious, and political" were the words used by eighteenth-century judge Thomas Jones to describe the Mohawk Indian woman, Molly Brant.[1] To Jones, they summarized the character and role of this important and influential woman. She was helpmate and partner to one of the most powerful white men of the eighteenth century as well as the mother of eight of his children. She was a vital link between the white world and that of the Six Nations of the Iroquois before, during, and after the American Revolution. The judge's account is only one of many documenting her roles as mother, diplomat, and Mohawk matron.

Molly Brant lived an unusually full, active and influential life for any woman of the eighteenth century. She was a complex person, the product of a Native American society that was adapting to the encroachments of the white world upon its traditional homeland. While willingly embracing the comforts and social life of that world, she did not abandon her own cultural identity. Her contemporaries at times described her as "prudent," "delightful," or "agreeable" and at others as "scolding," "a trouble maker," or a woman with "a violent temper." She raised eight children to be at home in both worlds. Due to her political beliefs, her children experienced eight years of dislocation and turmoil. During that time, Brant's grit and determination enabled her to succeed in her political role, keep her household together, see to her children's education, and recover some of their lost inheritance.

Molly Brant made choices for which she is sometimes criticized today. Some have even seen her as having played a major role in the loss of Iroquois land in New York State, because of her efforts to help maintain their loyalty to the British. It can be said that her political persuasiveness influenced the decisions of the Six Nations in matters she thought best both for them and for herself.

Providing for her family was also a priority. Brant and her children adopted a material culture befitting their status. She sent them to English schools, but they could also read, write and speak Mohawk. She could act

---

[1] Edward Floyd De Lancey (ed.), *History of New York During the Revolutionary War, and the Leading Events in the Other Colonies at that Period, by Thomas Jones, Justice of the Supreme Court of the Province* (2 vols.; New York: 1879), II, p. 374. De Lancey's work was produced from Jones' original hand-written manuscript, which was believed to have been written between 1783 and 1788. The 2-volume set was edited by De Lancey for the New-York Historical Society. Jones' manuscript was based on his memoirs, begun while under house arrest on Long Island during the Revolution.

as proper hostess to the local visitor as well as the visiting colonial élite, and was not shy about speaking her opinion in the company of authority, white or Indian.

Some of Molly Brant's political power came from her family connections. Her stepfather, Brant Canagaraduncka, was an important Mohawk sachem; Sir William Johnson, her consort, supervised British-Indian affairs in the northern colonies; her brother Joseph was an important military and political figure during and after the American Revolution. But Molly Brant was also the product of a matrilineal society where women were respected and consulted and held real power. She carried this influence and training into Sir William's household where she acted as one of his important contacts with the Indian groups living north and west of their home. Judge Jones concluded that "through her means he was always enabled to gain the most authentic intelligence, and to counteract every scheme undertaken by his enemies to set up the Indians against him."[2] Indeed, she was a power broker. Brant merged her considerable abilities with the influence uniquely available to her through her male connections to become a powerful political person in her own right. Before the age of forty she was a prominent figure well-known even to American officers during the Revolutionary War. At the same time, she maintained her domestic sphere. Left to raise eight children, who ranged in age from one to fifteen when Sir William Johnson died in 1774, she was determined to see that they should keep their rightful inheritance, a task to which she devoted several years of her life.

Still foremost in the minds of those who have studied Molly Brant's life is the question of her marriage bond with Sir William Johnson. It was not viewed as legitimate under English law. In 1818 their son, George, petitioned against a court decision barring his claim to land belonging to his deceased sister because "the marriage of their said Father and Mother, although acknowledged and avowed by them, and conformable to the usages of the Nation to which she belonged, was defective in point of legal form."[3] Brant and Johnson, however, lived together for more than fifteen years as man and wife. Theirs was not a clandestine but a highly public relationship. They worked together both in the running of a busy household and as a political force in colonial New York.

This study seeks to present a broad view of Molly Brant as woman and mother as well as power broker. It incorporates primary and unpublished sources previously untapped, including information on the material culture of her comfortable lifestyle. Sadly, her story over the years has been overshadowed by that of Sir William and even her brother, Joseph. Obscurity did not befall Molly during her lifetime nor should it occur now.

---

[2] *Ibid.*

[3] Petition of George Johnson to Sir Peregrine Maitland, Sept. 1, 1818, *Upper Canada Land Petitions,* National Archives of Canada, Ottawa, Reel C2110, R.G. 1, L3, Vol. 256, transcribed by Paul Huey.

Rather, she deserves recognition for her achievements in the face of overwhelming odds. Few women in the eighteenth century could have accomplished as much. Although she is honored in English Canada as one of its founders, her story is not well known in the United States. And yet what a fascinating tale it is!

Sir William Johnson's Coat-of-Arms.
Engraving, after Johnson, by D.S. Knight.

Sir Peter Warren, mentor to William Johnson and Vice-Admiral in the Royal Navy. *Courtesy, The National Maritime Museum, London.*

Chapter One
CANAJOHARIE AND FORT JOHNSON

Molly Brant was born about 1736 to Christian Mohawk parents. This date is based on a 1783 record in which she then declared herself to be forty-seven years of age.[4] However, the baptismal records of the church at Fort Hunter, New York, for April 13, 1735 list a child, Mary, daughter of Margaret and Cannassware.[5] If this was Molly Brant, she had a different father than her younger brother, Joseph, who was born in 1743. Since lineage among the Iroquois is matrilineal, however, having the same mother made them siblings. Molly's Mohawk name was "Kon?watsi?tsiai e n?ni" or "Gonwatsijayenni," meaning "someone lends her a flower."[6] She was a member of the Wolf clan.

Molly Brant reached maturity at what was known as "the "Upper Castle," the Indian town of Canajoharie. Europeans, from an early date, commonly referred to fortified Indian villages as "castles," and the term continued to be used throughout the colonial period. This was at a different location than the present–day village of Canajoharie. The Indian town was located on the south side of the Mohawk River, thirty miles upstream from "the Lower Castle," called Tionderoga, located next to Fort Hunter. By Brant's time both Mohawk settlements were surrounded by white farmers and traders, among them one William Johnson. Johnson emigrated from Ireland in 1738 to develop land in the Mohawk Valley on behalf of his uncle, Peter Warren, later an admiral in the Royal Navy.

Born in 1715 of lesser gentry, William Johnson left his family some twenty-three years later, never to return. Tremendously ambitious, he led settlers to his uncle's land claim, established farms and a trading post, and proceeded to acquire property, influence and political power in his own right. One element of Johnson's success was his shrewd partnership with the Mohawk at Tionderoga and Canajoharie. Only a year after his arrival, correspondence between William and his uncle shows that he was already closely involved with the local Indians and could report that "the Cheifs ...

---

[4] Return of Loyalists on Carleton Island, Nov. 26, 1783, *Frederick Haldimand Papers,* Add. MSS 21787, British Library, London. From microfilm copies in the National Archives of Canada, Ottawa, Reel A689, MSS 21787, p. 344, transcribed by Paul Huey. British Library reference numbers will be used hereafter.

[5] Isabel Thompson Kelsay, *Joseph Brant, 1743-1807: Man of Two Worlds* (Syracuse, NY: 1984), p. 40.

[6] Barbara Graymont, "Konwatsi?tsiaiénni," *Dictionary of Canadian Biography,* IV (Toronto: 1979), p. 416. The "?" is the linguistic symbol for a glottal stop.

Sir William Johnson, in a painting by John Wollaston, c.1751. *Courtesy, Albany Institute of History & Art.*

were so well pleased at my <Settleing> [sic] here, and keeping wt. [what] necessarrys they wanted."[7] Johnson demonstrated his influence at the Indian conference held in Albany in 1746 where he appeared at the head of the Mohawk delegation "dressed and painted after the Manner of an Indian War-Captain."[8] He was not unknown to the colonial delegation gathered in Albany, for he had been appointed Justice of the Peace in 1745.[9] It was also not uncommon in the colonial period for Europeans to dress as Indians as many, even colonial governors, followed Indian customs of speech and gift-giving during conferences.[10] After Johnson's military victory at the Battle of Lake George in 1755, his status grew even more when he was made a baronet by King George II. Johnson's success in enlisting the Mohawk against the French eventually led to his appointment, in 1756, as Superintendent of Indian Affairs for the Northern District, a powerful position he held until his death in 1774. In 1767 Johnson declared in a letter to the Earl of Shelburne that "I have always made use of a few approved Chiefs of the several Nations."[11] By consulting and giving large quantities of gifts to important sachems, Johnson became a power broker in the affairs of both the upper and lower Mohawk communities. The Brant family was one of those he dealt with most.

The people living in the two major Mohawk towns had, by the 1750s, gradually adopted new customs due to the pressure of white settlers surrounding them, and as a result of the steady decline in population that had occurred. Disease, warfare, and religious differences took their toll, leaving fewer native inhabitants residing in the Valley. One estimate suggests that two-thirds of the Mohawk had gone to Canada to live at the Roman Catholic mission villages on the St. Lawrence River at Kanawake, Kanesatake, Akwesasne, and Oswegatchie. Diseases, such as smallpox and measles, had devastating effects on the remaining inhabitants. Warfare accelerated the decline, although casualties were sometimes replaced through the assimilation of captives. Adopting captives into the tribe was not at all unusual. During warfare against the French, however, it was expected that prisoners taken in support of British military operations would be surrendered to Crown authority.

---

[7] Sir William Johnson to Peter Warren, May 10, 1739, James Sullivan, Alexander C. Flick and Milton W. Hamilton (eds.), *The Papers of Sir William Johnson* (cited hereafter as *SWJP;* 14 vols.; Albany: 1921-65), I, p. 6.

[8] Cadwallader Colden, *The History of the Five Indian Nations of Canada* (2 vols.; Toronto: 1902), II, pp. 220-21. Colden was present at the Albany conference.

[9] Milton W. Hamilton, *Sir William Johnson, Colonial American, 1715-1763* (Port Washington, NY: 1976), p. 44.

[10] *Ibid.,* p. 342.

[11] Sir William Johnson to the Earl of Shelburne, Aug. 17, 1767, E.B. O'Callaghan and B. Fernow (eds.), *Documents Relative to the Colonial History of the State of New York* (cited hereafter as *DRCHSNY;* 15 vols.; Albany: 1853–87), VII, p. 946.

Fort Johnson. *Courtesy, New York State Office of Parks, Recreation and Historic Preservation; Johnson Hall State Historic Site.*

Fort Johnson. Engraving by Hulett, of a drawing by Guy Johnson, from *Royal Magazine* **for 1759, p. 167.**

Extended families, residing communally in the traditional longhouse setting, gradually moved toward a single-family nuclear structure, living in small houses. Corn fields were now plowed and fenced, a service provided by local settlers through Sir William Johnson. By 1747, Johnson had a blockhouse built to protect the Mohawk at Canajoharie. By 1755, a fort had been constructed there as well. Colonial forces manned both military installations. This sometimes led to conflicts of authority between the military leaders and sachems as well as other annoyances such as the garrison cattle getting into Indian fields and destroying crops. Despite these problems, inhabitants needed protection, especially while the men were away hunting, working, or making war.

Hunting was less important now that domestic animals such as cattle, hogs and poultry were being kept for food by the inhabitants. Fur trade had also decreased in importance. Pelts were still sought, but with greater difficulty, as it became necessary to travel farther west to find fur-bearing animals. Many men worked for wages at tasks such as transporting bateaux, messenger service and, especially, military duty. The last included spying on the enemy, serving in raiding parties and marching with English troops to major encounters.

Protected by soldiers from the fortifications, women tended crops and were also paid in cash for making moccasins, leggings and additional clothing, as well as carrying messages. On more than one occasion, Johnson clothed all of the women and children of Canajoharie. His expense accounts for this activity in November 1758 record seventy-six women and eighty-nine children present at Canajoharie while the men were away. In addition to clothing them, he promised to furnish provisions, "they being quite destitute of any thing in Store."[12] These 165 individuals represented perhaps two-thirds of the town's residents, indicating it was a small place.

Even if the population of Fort Hunter (Lower Castle) and lesser Mohawk hamlets in the area were of equal size, total numbers of Mohawk by this time period would have been about 500 individuals compared to an estimated 4,550 German and Dutch settlers living around them.[13] Colonial New Yorkers took great care not to offend the Mohawk, having realized the extent of their considerable power, importance as useful workers, holders of vast tracts of land, and skilled warriors. As members of the powerful Iroquois Confederation, the Mohawk could call upon their allies for assistance. In a more gradual population decline than the Mohawk, these more distant nations showed a lesser degree of European cultural influence; therefore, the Oneida, Cayuga, Onondaga, Seneca, and Tuscarora were considered by colonists to be less "civilized." When conferences were convened by colonial authorities, both Iroquois men and women attended. At these gatherings they received many presents, as rewards for attending

---

[12] Journal of Indian Affairs, Oct. 31-Nov. 10, 1758, *SWJP,* X, p. 53.

[13] David B. Guldenzopf, "The Colonial Transformation of Mohawk Iroquois Society." Unpublished PhD. dissertation, Department of Anthropology, State University of New York at Albany, 1986, pp. 67, 55.

Reverend John Ogilvie, by John S. Copley. *Courtesy, The Parish of Trinity Church.*

and in recognition of their custom of reciprocity. Participants were also given shelter and food to help compensate for the disruption to their domestic affairs resulting from attendance at these councils.

Numerous attempts had been made to Christianize the Mohawk and to teach the children to read and write in their own language. Persuading them to accept the Christian religion was a long process. In 1717, when missionaries began to preach at Canajoharie, some inhabitants marched back and forth beating a drum to drown out their words![14] By the 1750s, however, most villagers had been baptized in the Anglican Church. Partial success in this endeavor is exemplified by Molly Brant's mother, Margaret. She was apparently a practicing Anglican. In 1753, she had a new baby baptized, and the Reverend John Ogilvie recorded the child in the baptismal record as "Jacob son of Margt. the Widow of Lykas by Brandt of Canijohare."[15] Six months later Margaret and Brant were married, the child having apparently died. However, the fact that Margaret, in the eyes of the Anglican clergy, had committed adultery with Brant before their marriage resulted in her being kept from taking communion in the church. Therefore, to be reinstated, on February 17, 1754, she made a "Humble Confession in Publick, for the heinous Sin of Adultery, for which Crime she had been put off from the Comunion for a considerable Time past."[16] This confession must have been a difficult thing for Margaret to do. Her daughter Molly was about eighteen years old at the time, and Joseph was eleven. Both children were devout Anglicans in later life. Perhaps they helped persuade their mother that her act of contrition was necessary.

By 1769, Sir William Johnson had built an Anglican church at Canajoharie. A school for children established at Fort Hunter in 1713 served all the local communities, so that by the middle of the eighteenth century many Mohawk children had some exposure to reading and writing. Molly and Joseph must have received some of this training, because both could read and write Mohawk.

Thus, Molly Brant grew up in a world quite different from that of her ancestors. The Mohawk adapted to change by accepting those practices that seemed to make their lives better. They maintained traditions and beliefs, and grafted to them new ideas that proved useful. The longhouse did not disappear, as families moved to small houses, but became the center for ceremonial life. Guns largely replaced the bow and arrow. Copper kettles proved more durable than clay pots. Cloth obtained from the traders was more easily sewn into clothing. Domestic animals helped supplement the food supply. These adaptations were occurring throughout Iroquoia,

---

[14] James Axtell, *The Invasion Within: The Contest of Cultures in Colonial North America* (New York: 1985), p. 262.

[15] Kelsay, p. 53.

[16] Milton W. Hamilton (ed.), "The Diary of the Reverend John Ogilvie, 1750-1759," *The Bulletin of the Fort Ticonderoga Museum*, X, No. 5 (February 1961), p. 342.

but the Mohawk, located closest to white settlements, had embraced them to a greater extent by the 1750s than others in the Confederacy.

One institution that did not change was the important role women played in Iroquois society. Through their matrilineages, women controlled the lands, lodges and wealth of the family. Military and political leaders were chosen from the male population. Clan Mothers selected individuals from certain hereditary lineages to become sachems. These women could also depose a sachem they thought was not fulfilling his responsibilities. Such decisions undoubtedly were made with knowledge of what the rest of the tribe would accept, but clan matrons had the final say. Women were consulted about policy, particularly when war was contemplated. They expressed their opinions at local councils, and their views were conveyed through male representatives to the Confederacy's central council at Onondaga.[17] The significant role of women in Iroquois society was well known and often observed by colonials. Sir William's brother, Warren Johnson, wrote in his journal while visiting from Ireland that "the Indian women have very great Influence over the Indians, soe that if the young Warriours are going to War they can almost hinder them. but when going ... [they] get a charge from the Old Women, particularly to behave well, & not to be a Discredit to themselves, or their forefathers."[18] Margaret Brant was not born to one of the important lineages from which sachems were chosen. Her children were not to inherit that kind of influence. However, Iroquoian society allowed people of extraordinary ability to rise to other positions of power. Both Joseph and Molly Brant would do so.

By 1754, and probably before, Molly Brant lived in the best house in Canajoharie due to her mother's marriage to the important Mohawk sachem, Brant Canagaraduncka.[19] Archaeological excavations at the site of this house, later occupied by Joseph Brant, have revealed that it was a substantial structure with a stone cellar, clapboarded exterior walls joined by hand-wrought nails, a fireplace, glass windows, plaster interior walls, and outbuildings, including a large Dutch barn and a smaller wooden building that perhaps functioned as a summer kitchen.[20] Although im-

---

[17] For modern discussions, see Nancy Bonvillain, "Iroquoian Women," in Nancy Bonvillain (ed.), *Studies on Iroquoian Culture* (Rindge, NH: 1980), pp. 47–80; James Axtell (ed.), *The Indian Peoples of Eastern America: A Documentary History of the Sexes* (New York: 1981), pp. 150–66; Gretchen M. Bataille and Kathleen Mullen Sands (eds.), *American Indian Women Telling Their Lives* (Lincoln, NB: 1984), p. 18; June Namias, *White Captive: Gender and Ethnicity on the American Frontier* (Chapel Hill, NC: 1993); W.G. Spittal (ed.), *Iroquois Women: An Anthology* (Ohsweken, ON: 1990).

[18] Journal of Warren Johnson, June 29, 1760-July 3, 1761, *SWJP*, XIII, p. 192.

[19] For a description of Indian cabins as early as 1743, see John Bartram's reports in Helen Gere Cruickshank (ed.), *John and William Bartram's America* (Garden City, NY: 1961), pp. 23–42; John Christopher Guzzardo, "Sir William Johnson's Official Family: Patron and Clients in an Anglo-American Empire, 1742-1777." Unpublished PhD. dissertation, Department of History, Syracuse University, 1975, pp. 258-62; Kelsay, pp. 52-54.

[20] Guldenzopf, pp. 104-12.

provements were undoubtedly made later, the basic form, that of a Dutch-style house, dates to its initial construction. Sachem Brant had "a horse and wagon, some fat cows, and a pretty good house, and he could sign his name."[21] Standing on the property today is a large Dutch barn, probably constructed at or near the same time as the house and used to shelter Brant's crops and perhaps, at times, his horse, cows and wagon. Molly Brant did not join Sir William Johnson "as a forest child of simple, untutored graces" who experienced an "astonishing evolution" as "wigwam housekeeping has never been noted for neatness" as some historians have maintained.[22] She came well acquainted with European-style architecture and household goods, having traveled to Philadelphia in 1754 with her step-father. They, and other Mohawk, were accompanied there by Daniel Claus. While in Albany, on the return journey, Claus reported that a military officer "fell in Love with Ms Mary Brant who was then Likely."[23] Brant knew much of the world outside her village before she joined Sir William at his home known as Fort Johnson.

Since Sir William always stayed at the Brant house in Canajoharie when he visited the Upper Castle, he must have known "Miss Molly" for some years.[24] A widely believed but unsubstantiated story is that he first saw her at a militia muster when "she leaped upon" a mounted officer's horse "with the agility of a gazelle ... and clinging to the officer, her blanket flying, and her dark tresses streaming in the wind, she flew about the parade ground swift as an arrow."[25] Regardless of how they met, Molly Brant was a presence in Sir William's household by 1759. In September of that year she gave birth to their first child, Peter Warren Johnson. The boy was named after his father's uncle and original patron.

William Johnson already had three children by Catherine Weissenberg, a German who had been a runaway indentured servant, clearly a woman of spirit and determination. However, by April 1759 Johnson was ordering mourning materials while a friend wrote, "When I left you I thought there appeared little hopes of Mss. [sic] Katys Life. I condole with you there-upon."[26] Apparently, she died that spring. Unlike Molly, Catherine Weissenberg's name does not appear in Johnson's papers as an influence

---

[21] Kelsay, p. 51.

[22] Arthur Pound, *Johnson of the Mohawks* (New York: 1930), p. 141.

[23] *Memo Book, Claus Papers,* National Archives of Canada, Ottawa, Reel C1485, 23, 36–37, transcribed by Wanda Burch.

[24] Kelsay, p. 67; Guzzardo, p. 260.

[25] William L. Stone, *The Life and Times of Sir William Johnson, Bart.* (2 vols.; Albany: 1865), I, pp. 327–328n.

[26] Capt. Peter Wraxall to Sir William Johnson, May 23, 1759, E.B. O'Callaghan (ed.), *The Documentary History of the State of New-York* (Cited hereafter as *DHNY;* 4 vols.; Albany: 1849-51), II, p. 785.

**Traditionally thought to be
Colonel Daniel Claus;
protégé, aide
and
son-in-law of
Sir William Johnson.
However, based on the early
nineteenth-century style of
clothing, this is probably
his son William.**
*Courtesy, National Archives of Canada,
Ottawa.*

**Ann (Nancy) Johnson Claus;
daughter of
Sir William Johnson
and
Catherine Weissenberg,
and
wife of Daniel Claus.**
*Courtesy, National Archives of Canada,
Ottawa.*

**Daniel Claus and Molly Brant were great correspondents, and much information
about her comes from his papers.**

in his affairs. She is not recorded as having made purchases nor as being thanked by guests for her services as hostess. Catherine was remembered by Sir William in his will as "my beloved wife." She was the mother of his son John and two daughters, Ann (Nancy) and Mary (Polly). Ann later married Johnson's close aide, Daniel Claus, and Mary wed his nephew, Guy Johnson. All three, in their teens and twenties by 1759, lived at Fort Johnson with Molly Brant and their father until Johnson Hall was constructed in 1763. Although Ann was married in 1762 and Mary in 1763, their husbands were frequently away, so they continued to reside at Fort Johnson until their own homes were ready in 1766. John Johnson remained at Fort Johnson until his father's death in 1774.

Molly Brant was in her early twenties by 1759, and Sir William was in his forties. More children followed Peter, though precise dates remain in doubt. One contemporary source suggests that Molly gave birth to Elizabeth in 1763, while still at Fort Johnson, and to the others, at Johnson Hall, as follows: Magdalene, 1765; Margaret, 1767; George, 1769; Mary, 1771; Susanna, 1772; and Anne, 1773.[27]

Molly Brant brought more than children to the union with Johnson. Sir William once explained that her brother Joseph would be useful because of his "connection and residence" at Canajoharie.[28] He must have viewed Molly in a similar light. Sir William did not make a list of suitable heiresses to marry in order to expand his wealth and social standing, as he did for his son John years later.[29] But Molly Brant was someone he needed in his world. Personal and professional success depended upon his ability to maintain good relations with the Iroquois, a fact which must have brought considerable tension to his daily life. She helped Johnson maintain these important connections.

For her part, although as Judge Jones observed, "she loved Sir William to adoration,"[30] Molly also recognized that his access to power, influence, and money could provide a better life for her and her future children. For his part, Sir William "lived with her in all the intimacy of the most conjugal affection."[31] Johnson noted in his will that he and Molly had shared a "long and uninterrupted friendship."[32]

---

[27] Return of Loyalists on Carleton Island, Nov. 26, 1783, *Haldimand Papers,* Add. MSS 21787, p.344. It should be noted that while the birth years shown are based on this document, William Johnson makes note in his "Journal To Detroit" (July 4-Oct. 30, 1761) that he was informed in October of Molly having delivered a girl. *SWJP,* XIII, p. 271.

[28] Sir William Johnson to the Lords of Trade, Nov. 13, 1763, *DRCHSNY,* VII, p. 580.

[29] Sir William Johnson to Thomas Moncrieffe, March 16, 1771; Moncrieffe to Johnson, March 4, 1773, *SWJP,* VIII, pp. 24-25, 729.

[30] Jones' History in De Lancey, Vol. II, p. 374.

[31] *Ibid.*

[32] Will of Sir William Johnson, Jan. 27, 1774, *SWJP,* XII, p. 1075.

Johnson Hall. *Courtesy, New York State Office of Parks, Recreation and Historic Preservation; Johnson Hall State Historic Site.*

Chapter Two
JOHNSON HALL

Molly Brant had probably been a force in Indian affairs from the very beginning of her relationship with Johnson, but it was at Johnson Hall that she became visible as housekeeper and hostess. "Sensible" and "judicious"[33] and a "prudent & faithfull Housekeeper,"[34] she was in charge of a busy household. Johnson had slaves, a cook, gardener, farm overseer, secretary, and bookkeeper to perform daily household tasks. In the eighteenth century, a "housekeeper" was defined as "one who keeps a good, beautiful, etc. house; a hospitable person; a person in charge of a house, office, place of business, etc., and a woman who manages or superintends the affairs of a household; esp. the woman in control of the female servants of a household."[35]

While all of these duties pertain to Brant's situation, the last seems most germane. Contemporary accounts record her making purchases of such items as a dozen creamware cups and saucers (tea ware), an iron skillet and countless sewing items at the local store and from merchants in Schenectady and Butlersbury.[36] She and Sir William were hosts to many visitors. New York Governors Henry Moore and William Tryon, William Franklin of New Jersey, as well as John Penn and Chief Justice William Allen of Pennsylvania were among them. So too were Lord Adam Gordon and Lady Susan O'Brien from England. All of these elite guests, to name but a few, brought their attendants and, sometimes, families.[37] Judge Thomas Jones, Justice of the Supreme Court of New York Colony and a friend, described a typical day as "a kind of open house" in which the couple played host to travelers from all parts of America, Europe and the West Indies:

> *The gentlemen and ladies breakfasted in their respec-*
> *tive rooms, and, at their option, had either tea, coffee, or*
> *chocolate, or if an old rugged veteran wanted a beef steak,*

---

[33] Jones' History in De Lancey, Vol. II, pp. 374.

[34] *Ibid.,* p. 1070.

[35] *The Compact Edition of the Oxford English Dictionary* (2 vols.; Glasgow: 1971), I, p. 1340.

[36] Robert Adems Day Book, June 10, 1768-July 14, 1773, *SWJP,* XIII, pp. 532-616; John Butler Account Book, Sept. 25, 1761-Oct. 13, 1771, *SWJP,* XIII, pp. 506-32; *Daniel Campbell Ledgers, Campbell Family Papers,* 23 boxes, New York State Library, Albany

[37] Milton W. Hamilton, *Sir William Johnson and the Indians of New York* (Albany: 1975), p. 35.

a mug of ale, a glass of brandy, or some grog, he called for it, and it always was at his service. The freer people made, the more happy was Sir William. After breakfast, while Sir William was about his business, his guests entertained themselves as they pleased. Some rode out, some went out with guns, some with fishing-tackle, some sauntered about the town, some played cards, some backgammon, some billiards, some pennies, and some even at nine-pins. Thus was each day spent until the hour of four, when the bell punctually rang for dinner, and all assembled. He had besides his own family, seldom less than ten, sometimes thirty. All were welcome. All sat down together. All was good cheer, mirth, and festivity. Sometimes seven, eight, or ten, of the Indian Sachems joined the festive board. His dinners were plentiful. They consisted, however, of the produce of his estate, or what was procured from the woods and rivers, such as venison, bear, and fish of every kind, with wild turkeys, partridges, grouse, and quails in abundance. No jellies, creams, ragouts, or sillibubs graced his table. His liquors were Madeira, ale, strong beer, cider, and punch. Each guest chose what he liked, and drank as he pleased. The company, or at least a part of them, seldom broke up before three in the morning. Every one, however, Sir William included, retired when he pleased. There was no restraint.[38]

Molly Brant was responsible for providing hospitality to visitors, and perhaps the type of food served was a reflection of her own background and tastes. That she participated as hostess is shown by thank-you notes and gifts from guests such as Lord Adam Gordon who, after a visit in 1765, wrote "my Love to Molly & thanks for her good Breakfast."[39] Another visitor shamefacedly apologized "Sorry I did not take Leave of Miss Molly-I begg Sir ... be pleased to Assure her, that it was not for want of [manners but?] the Effect of Stupidity."[40] John van Eps sent a leg of venison specifically for her. George Croghan and Normand MacLeod each dispatched gifts: the former, trinkets from London for Molly and the children; the latter, two blankets from Niagara.[41] Witham Marsh forwarded compliments and called her by a contraction of her Indian name, probably an affectionate

---

[38] Jones' History in De Lancey, Vol. II, pp. 373-74.

[39] Lord Adam Gordon to Sir William Johnson, July 2, 1765; *SWJP*, XIII, p. 376.

[40] John Wetherhead to Sir William Johnson, Nov. 17, 1768, *SWJP*, VI, p. 463.

[41] John B. Van Eps to Sir William Johnson, Feb. 21, 1770, *SWJP*, VII, p. 409; George Croghan to Sir William Johnson, Aug. 4, 1764, *SWJP*, IV, p. 501; Normand MacLeod to Sir William Johnson, Jan. 23, 1769, *SWJP*, VI, p. 604.

nickname, "chgiagh."[42] Other visitors included military officers, land speculators, members of St. Patrick's Masonic Lodge which was headquartered at Johnson Hall and even a blind Irish harpist, John Kain.[43] The pastor of St. Peter's Anglican Church in Albany recorded his trips to the Hall for the purpose of baptizing children, at least one of whom was Brant's. Probably some of the others were also, based on a comparison of his entries with estimates of their birth dates.[44]

In addition to her own children, two boys, fathered by Sir William with now-unknown Indian women prior to Brant's first pregnancy, probably were frequent visitors. Brant Johnson was born in the 1740s and William of Canajoharie in the 1750s.[45] Both were given inheritances by Johnson in his will. Years later, Molly Brant referred to William of Canajoharie as her "son," indicating she probably had something to do with his upbringing, or that in Iroquois terms, he was related to her through his mother. Joseph Brant was sent by Johnson to Reverend Eleazar Wheelock's school for Indians in Connecticut, and he visited his sister on occasion, along with his mother, stepfather and other family and friends from Canajoharie.

Sir William held frequent Indian councils at Johnson Hall. Between 1763 and 1774, when he died speaking at one such event, there were at least twelve official conferences and numerous meetings.[46] Indeed, more than once, Johnson groaned, "I have ... every Room & Corner in my House Constantly full of Indians."[47] Hundreds came from all over the northern colonies to attend these gatherings. All needed to be housed, fed and given presents, along with reassurances of the British government's support and friendship. Molly Brant's role in all of this is obvious. Years later, a traveler in Canada reported that she "has always been a faithful and useful friend in Indian affairs, while she resided in Johnston [sic] hall, and since her removal to Upper Canada ... When treaties or purchases were about to be made at Johnston hall, she has often persuaded the obstinate chiefs into a compliance with the proposals for peace, or sale of lands."[48] It is possible

---

[42] Witham Marsh to Sir William Johnson, Feb. 19, 1764, *SWJP,* XI, p. 72.

[43] James F. Dunne and Lucy McCaffery, "O'Cahan: The Blind Harper of Johnson Hall," *Folk Harp Journal,* No. 47 (December 1984); Francis Wade to Sir William Johnson, March 25, 1771, and Wade to Johnson, April 30, 1771, *SWJP,* VIII, pp. 42, 91.

[44] Records of St. Peter's Church, Albany, New York, 1769-1770, II (1768–1775), New York State Library, pp. 101–03.

[45] Kelsay, p. 68.

[46] Chronology and Itinerary for Sir William Johnson, 1715-1774, *SWJP,* I, pp. xxv–xxxiii.

[47] Sir William Johnson to Thomas Gage, March 16, 1764, *SWJP,* IV, p. 370; Johnson to George Croghan, March 5, 1768, *SWJP,* XII, p. 461; Johnson to John Watts, April 5, 1768, *SWJP,* VI, p. 178; Johnson to Gage, April 8, 1768, *Ibid.,* p. 184.

[48] John C. Ogden, A *Tour Through Upper and Lower Canada* (Wilmington, DE: 1800), p. 61.

Indian Conference at Johnson Hall, as portrayed in a twentieth-century oil painting by Edward L. Henry. *Courtesy, Albany Institute of History & Art.*

that some Indians were pleased to see one of their own, along with her children, living with Johnson. At the same time, Brant increased her own power among these groups as a person to be consulted. She would maintain and augment this power in the years ahead.

An insight into one of her roles is offered by an exchange of letters with Captain James Stevenson, a fur trader, former military officer and Indian agent who lived in Albany. While commandant of Fort Niagara, Stevenson had fathered a son with a Seneca woman and was interested in purchasing the boy from the Seneca. Stevenson requested Molly Brant's advice and help. Later, he thanked both William and Molly for the pains they took, although the outcome remains unclear. In another case, Stevenson asked her to flatter an Indian whom he saw as a rising star in his nation.[49]

Brant also watched over Johnson's interests while he was away from home, occasionally attending Indian conferences held in places as distant as Detroit, at other times traveling on private business. Between 1759 and 1774, Johnson was gone (at a conservative estimate) over twenty percent of the time, sometimes for as long as two months.[50] During these periods, crops had to be tended and harvested, tenants' complaints addressed, and wagonloads of food and trade goods inspected. When Indian conferences were planned, entire wagon trains of supplies were sent from nearby urban centers. The logistics of such undertakings must have been overwhelming. Although Brant's world was the domestic sphere, she undoubtedly kept a watchful eye on all of these matters as well. At the same time, she longed to take her place by his side. In the midst of building a new fort at Oswego, Johnson had to write a letter to Molly telling her to stay home.[51] This was in August 1759, a month before Peter was born.

By the end of the 1760s, Sir William's health was beginning to deteriorate. Suffering from an old wound received at the Battle of Lake George, which left a musket ball in his leg, and worn out by constant travel and a strenuous life, Johnson was frequently ill.[52] Brant, known in later years as a healer, no doubt cared for Sir William during these periods, adding to her many other duties.

Archaeological excavations at Johnson Hall have demonstrated that the material culture of the household included the finest European goods then available in colonial New York. Tea services and tablewares of porcelain,

---

[49] James Stevenson to Sir William Johnson, Dec. 25, 1773, *SWJP,* VIII, p. 974; Stevenson to Johnson, March 13, 1771, *Ibid.,* p 16, Stevenson to Johnson, May 8, 1772, *Ibid.,* p. 469; Stevenson to Johnson, March 31, 1774, *Ibid.,* p. 1103; Stevenson to Johnson, April 1, 1774, *Ibid.,* pp. 1107-08.

[50] Chronology and Itinerary for Sir William Johnson, 1715-1774, *SWJP,* I, pp. xxv–xxxiii.

[51] Journal of Niagara Campaign, July 26-Oct. 14, 1759, *SWJP,* XIII, p. 125.

[52] Wanda Burch, "Sir William Johnson and Eighteenth-Century Medicine in the New York Colony," in Peter Benes (ed.), *Medicine and Health: The Annual Proceedings of the Dublin Seminar for New England Folklife* (Boston: 1990). Burch is Site Manager at Johnson Hall State Historic Site, Johnstown, New York.

Mantlepiece in the formal Blue Parlor of Johnson Hall; adorned in accordance with documentary and archaeological evidence, resembling the dual-cultural description noted in Joseph Bloomfield's journal of May 20, 1776. *Courtesy, New York State Office of Parks, Recreation and Historic Preservation; Johnson Hall State Historic Site.*

Left:
White salt-glazed stoneware excavated at Johnson Hall.
Courtesy, New York State Office of Parks, Recreation and Historic Preservation; Archaeology Unit, Peebles Island.

Right:
Shards of porcelain tableware excavated at Johnson Hall.
Courtesy, New York State Office of Parks, Recreation and Historic Preservation; Archaeology Unit, Peebles Island.

creamware and white salt-glazed stoneware have been found in abundance, along with crystal wine glasses and decanters. The 1774 inventory of the contents of the house included mahogany furniture, silver serving pieces and oil portraits. Added to these were numerous Indian items. Hung in the Hall, for example, were "3 Indn. Pictures, 2 white Deer Skins & do.fox." In the formal Blue Parlor was "a parcell of Indn. Trinkets over the Chimney."[53] Johnson was a well known collector of Native American artifacts.[54] A visitor in 1776 was shown "Sir Wm. Johnson's Picture, which was curiously surrounded with all kinds of Beads of Wamphum [sic], Indian curiositys and Trappings of Indian Finery wh. He had received in his Treatys with different Indian Nations, Curiositys sufficient to amuse the curious."[55] Thus, the home that Sir William Johnson and Molly Brant created contained evidence of both their cultures.

There are no known portraits of Brant, and descriptions of her personal appearance during this period are rare. Lady Susan O'Brien is reported to have remarked that she was a "well–bred and pleasant lady."[56] Anne Grant, then a child living in Albany, wrote years later that Molly Brant "possessed an uncommonly agreeable person, and good understanding."[57] Grant is not known to have met Brant, but she must have been repeating what she had heard from her elders.

Molly Brant's Loyalist claim for her losses as a result of the Revolutionary War, enumerated below, shows that she and her older daughters, at least on occasion, dressed in European clothing. Her claim includes chintz and silk for gowns, cotton and silk stockings, handkerchiefs, muslin aprons, hats, bonnets, silk gloves, cloth and leather shoes.[58] The list also carries three side-saddles, evidence that the females were riding English-style. Some of these items probably belonged to her daughters, the eldest of whom was by then fifteen, but the list documents the modes of dress of both Molly and her children. After leaving Johnson Hall, Brant was described as "dressed after the Indian Manner, but her linen and other Cloathes the

---

[53] An Inventory and Appraisal of the Furniture, Farming Utensils and Crop of the late Sir Wm. Johnson, Aug. 2, 1774, *SWJP,* XIII, pp. 652, 655.

[54] Wanda Burch, "Sir William Johnson's Cabinet of Curiosities," *New York History,* LXXI, No. 3 (July 1990), pp. 261-82.

[55] Journal of Joseph Bloomfield, May 20, 1776, in Mark E. Lender and James Kirby Martin (eds.), *Citizen Soldier: The Revolutionary War Journal of Joseph Bloomfield* (Newark, NJ: 1982), p. 49.

[56] Stone, II, p. 244; Charlotte Wilcoxen, "A Highborn Lady in Colonial New York," *The New-York Historical Society Quarterly,* LXIII, No. 4 (October 1979), p. 339. Stone said he quoted from a letter written by O'Brien. The letter has not been located since then.

[57] Anne Grant, *Memoirs of an American Lady: With Sketches of Manners and Scenes in America, as They Existed Previous to the Revolution* (Albany: 1876), p. 219.

[58] Guldenzopf, pp. 204–05.

Reverend Eleazar Wheelock, in a painting by Joseph Steward. Joseph Brant was one of the many who attended "Wheelock's School," as did his nephew, Peter. *Courtesy, Dartmouth College, Hood Museum of Art (original, oil-on-canvas; P.793.2). Commissioned by the Trustees of Dartmouth College, Hanover, New Hampshire.*

finest of their kind."[59] Indians had adopted European cloth and, sometimes, European clothing styles that they found attractive. In 1768, Joseph Brant and his first wife were reported wearing clothing made of English fabrics. He was dressed in a blue broadcloth, while she was in a calico or chintz gown.[60] A 1792 description of Joseph's third wife offers more detail as to how European fabrics were being used in a combination of styles. She was wearing a blanket, a jacket and a scanty petticoat of silk and fine English cloth with a lace border, leggings of scarlet that fit like stockings, and moccasins decorated with silk ribbons and beads.[61] At an Indian conference held in 1776 at German Flatts, Captain Joseph Bloomfield observed that sachems and their wives wore clothes made of fine fabrics but that the average Iroquois did not.[62] By this period, then, at least the elite among the Mohawk, both men and women, were dressing in fine fabrics sewn in a combination of European and native styles. Molly Brant dressed in the fashion of influential Mohawk, and sometimes in European clothes. In later life, she was consistently described as wearing a combination of both styles.

It is not known if Brant had an English education. Some historians suggest that she received schooling.[63] Johnson wrote letters to her while he was away from home.[64] Other contemporaries indicated she could write in Mohawk. Eleazar Wheelock, for example, noted that Joseph received a letter from Molly while at school, but Wheelock had not read it because he assumed it was in Mohawk.[65] In December 1778 the Mohawk leader, John Desorontyon, wrote to Claus in Mohawk quoting a letter he had received from Molly Brant written in the same language.[66]

The *Haldimand Papers* contain a letter "translated from Mary Brants letter to Col. Claus" dated Carleton Island April 12, 1781. The "translation" no doubt was from Mohawk to English. The letter (extant only in transla-

---

[59] Samuel Alexander Harrison (ed.), *Memoir of Lieut. Col. Tench Tilghman* (Albany: 1876), p. 87.

[60] Francis W. Halsey (ed.), *A Tour of Four Great Rivers: the Hudson, Mohawk, Susquehanna and Delaware in 1769; Being the Journal of Richard Smith of Burlington, New Jersey* (Port Washington, NY: 1964), p. 84.

[61] Patrick Campbell, *Travels in the Interior Inhabited Parts of North America in the Years 1791 and 1792.* Edited by H. H. Langton (Toronto: 1937), p. 164.

[62] Journal of Joseph Bloomfield, July 28, 1776, Lender and Martin, pp. 90–91.

[63] Earle Thomas, "Molly Brant," *Historic Kingston* (Kingston, ON: 1989:), p. 14; Graymont, "Konwatsi?tsiaiénni," p. 416; Gretchen Green, "Molly Brant, Catharine Brant, and Their Daughters: A Study in Colonial Acculturation", *Ontario History,* LXXXI, No. 3 (September 1989), p. 236.

[64] Journal of the Niagara Campaign, July 26-Oct. 14, 1759, *SWJP,* XIII, pp. 125, 139.

[65] Rev. Eleazar Wheelock fo Sir William Johnson, May 16, 1763, *DHNY,* IV, p. 330.

[66] H. Pearson Gundy, "Molly Brant - Loyalist," *Ontario History,* XIV, No. 3 (Summer 1953), p. 101. Gundy incorrectly states that Molly Brant's letter was donated to the Draper Collection, State Historical Society of Wisconsin, Madison. Instead, it was the one written by Desorontyon to Claus.

tion) is signed Mary Brant.[67] A receipt dated October 11, 1782, is signed "wari" (Mary) and the words "Mary Brant her mark" written around the letters. Unfortunately, this too is only a transcription done in John Johnson's hand.[68] Two Molly Brant letters in the *Claus Papers,* one dated 1778 and the other 1779, are in different hands. Each is of a flowery style quite unlike Claus's; either could be Molly's.[69] Barbara Graymont notes that Brant's letters, "if authentically from her own hand, show that she was mistress of a fine penmanship and a proper English style. There is some evidence, however, that she was only semi-literate and that the letters were dictated to an amanuensis."[70] Coming to a different conclusion, Earle Thomas wrote "the penmanship and syntax in her letters certainly would lead one to believe that she had been the recipient of some formal schooling; ... there are enough mistakes in them to lead one to believe [that she wrote them]."[71] Her children were educated, and it is possible that letters written in English were dictated to one of her daughters. Those written in Mohawk could have been written by Brant herself.

References to Molly's children are rare during the Johnson Hall period. Elizabeth (Betsy), like her mother, bought sewing materials at the local store.[72] Johnson established a school in nearby Johnstown for their education.[73] Teachers being hard to find, Peter sometimes was sent elsewhere, and it is about him that the most is known. After attending Wheelock's School, he went to Albany at the age of seven where he studied with the Anglican priest, Thomas Brown.[74] Brown promised to "take the same care of him in every Respect as my own child."[75] However, controversy

---

[67] Mary Brant to Daniel Claus, April 12, 1781, *Haldimand Papers,* Add. MSS 21774, p. 180.

[68] Receipt signed by Mary Brant, certified by John Johnson, Oct. 12, 1782, *Haldimand Papers,* Reel A684, p. 117. "Wari" is probably how the Mohawks pronounced "Mary" as their language has no "m."

[69] Mary Brant to Daniel Claus Oct. 5, 1779 and Brant to Claus, June 23, 1778, *Claus Papers,* MG19 F1, 2:39 and 135–36

[70] Graymont, "Konwatsi?tsiaiénni," p. 416.

[71] Thomas, p. 14.

[72] Extracts from the Phyn and Ellice Day Book, Aug. 19, 1767-Aug. 6, 1768, *SWJP,* XIII, pp. 590, 609, 613, 615.

[73] Johnson Calendar, April 9, 1765, *SWJP,* IV, p. 708; Thomas Barton to Sir William Johnson, Oct. 31, 1766, *SWJP,* V, p. 403; Samuel Auchmuty to Johnson, April 26, 1769, *SWJP,* VI, p. 710; Johnson to Auchmuty, Sept. 14, 1769, *SWJP,* VII, p. 169; John Cottgrave to Thomas Flood, Nov. 22, 1771, *SWJP,* VIII, p. 323; Cottgrave to Johnson, March 20, 1772, *Ibid.,* p. 424; Johnson Calendar, letter recorded from Cottgrave to Johnson, May 18, 1772, *Ibid.,* p 488; Johnson to Richard Hind, Nov. 25, 1773, *Ibid.,* p. 927; Hugh Gaine to Johnson, May 17, 1774, *Ibid.,* p. 1156.

[74] Eleazar Wheelock to Sir William Johnson, March 14, 1764, *SWJP,* XI, pp. 101-02.

[75] Rev. Thomas Brown to Sir William Johnson, Sept. 13, 1766, *DHNY,* IV, p. 233.

erupted over Brown's ministry, so Peter was sent to Schenectady where he probably attended a school run by St. George's Anglican Church.[76] This was perhaps the same school where Molly Brant sent her daughters after leaving Johnson Hall. When an education again became available in Johnstown, Peter was brought back home. There he became a favorite of his teacher, John Cottgrave. Before Peter left for further schooling in Montreal, Cottgrave asked Sir William's approval to give young Johnson some written instructions. In addition, Cottgrave asked "at Mr. Peters depart[ure] to present to him on my Account a 20/Bill as a Testimony for the Sence of his Bravery in the defence of the School House & from the Secred Simpathy I have in everything he dose."[77] Near Montreal, under the watchful eye of Daniel Claus, Peter lived with a French family, probably to learn the language. Those arrangements proved unsatisfactory, and he eventually moved into Montreal under the guidance of R. Huntley, a medical doctor and good friend of Johnson's nephew, Dr. John Dease.[78]

The next phase of Peter's education is well documented, and illustrated by his own correspondence. In 1773, only fourteen years old, Peter arrived in Philadelphia where he was to be trained in merchandising. On the way, escorted by Sir William's friend, Joseph Chew, he traveled by boat and stagecoach and dined in New York City with another of his father's associates, Hugh Wallace. In Philadelphia, Peter, perhaps somewhat homesick, was already asking for letters from family. He addressed his own correspondence to "Honored Father;" he promised to enclose others for "Mr. Dease" (a favorite of Peter's) and "to my Mother." He also asked for permission to buy a fiddle.[79] A month later, seemingly settled in, he wrote about his possible future and new violin, and sent respects to his mother, brother, sister, Dr. Dease and all friends at Johnson Hall.[80] In April 1774, Peter wrote two letters from Philadelphia. In one he asked that his love be given to his mother, and in the second he reminded her that he had written previously asking that she send him Indian curiosities to show to interested gentlemen and ladies. He requested a book written in Mohawk, "for I am Afraid I'll lose my Indian Toungue if I dont practice it more than I do." In addition, he asked for books in English and French to read during his

---

[76] Kevin Decker, church historian, confirmed that such a school was available at the church during the 1760s and 1770s.

[77] John Cottgrave to Sir William Johnson, March 20, 1772, *SWJP,* VIII, pp. 424-25.

[78] Daniel Claus Journal, July 1 and 12, 1773, *SWJP,* XIII, pp. 618, 621; Claus to Sir WIlliam Johnson, July 3, 1772, *SWJP,* VIII, pp. 524-27; Claus to Johnson, July 3, 1773, *Ibid.,* pp. 839-42; Claus to Johnson, Aug. 20, 1773, *Ibid.,* pp. 866-67; Johnson to Dr. R. Huntley, Feb. 14, 1774, *Ibid.,* pp. 1034-35; Huntley to Johnson, Jan. 2, 1773, *SWJP,* XII, p. 1010; Huntley to Johnson, March 3, 1773, *Ibid.,* p. 1013; Claus to Johnson, July 3, 1773, *Ibid.,* pp. 1026-29.

[79] Peter Johnson to Sir William Johnson, Nov. 18, 1773, *SWJP,* XII, pp. 1042–43.

[80] Peter Johnson to Sir William Johnson, Dec. 13, 1773, *SWJP,* VIII, p. 945.

Dining table setting at Johnson Hall; representation based on documentary and archaeological evidence. *Courtesy, New York State Office of Parks, Recreation and Historic Preservation; Johnson Hall State Historic Site.*

Dining table of Sir William Johnson (c. 1749-1763). This is a 'Gateleg' style table made of mahogany, with tulipwood drawer linings. It is in the collection of the Albany Institute of History & Art, and was the gift of the heirs of Major-General John Tayler Cooper. *Courtesy, Albany Institute of History & Art (1899.1).*

leisure hours. He enclosed a letter for sister Betsy and asked his father to write. A further request was made for a watch, so as to be more prompt. His attendance at a public hanging was also described.[81] Clearly, Peter was becoming a sophisticated and urbane gentleman, one who took pride in his Mohawk heritage. He was a favorite of his teachers, dined with his father's friends, wrote to his family, played the violin, read Mohawk, English and French, was interested in business and could live in large cities without fear. In addition, his sister Elizabeth could both read and write as could his mother to whom he sent separate letters, perhaps in Mohawk.

Molly Brant's busy domestic life at Johnson Hall came to an abrupt end with the death of Sir William in July 1774. Johnson's will left substantial bequests of land and money to her and each individual child. Her children received a total inheritance of £32,000, equal to the estate Johnson left his sons-in-law.[82] In the inventory of the contents of Johnson Hall in August 1774, Molly Brant's room was exempted as it contained her own personal belongings. Her later Loyalist claim gives some clues as to what these were. Although the list was made following her abrupt departure from Canajoharie, many of the items probably came with her from Johnson Hall and reveal the level of material culture to which she was accustomed. Her claim was the longest of any filed by displaced Mohawk from either castle.

Wary Gon wa tsi ja yenni[83]

New York Currency [£]
[pounds/shillings/pence]

4 Hair Trunks, 3 Large Leather D^O, 1 traveling D^O	8/-/-
4 Large Rose Blankets, 3 New Feather Beds	19/16/-
2 Old Feather Beds, 4 Green Rugs, 1 Cotton D^O	4/-/-
1 Coverlid, 4 Large Blankets, 6 French D^O	9/16/-
1 Large Beaver Blanket, 6 Pair Sheets	11/4/-
6 Pair Pillow Cases	1/4/-
40 Guineas, 40 Dollars & 6 half Joes [*]	109/17/4
*[Johannes-a Portugese gold coin]	
6 Silver Tablespoons, 2 Dozen Tea D^O, a Pair sugar tongs	24/3/-
2 Silver Mugs, 1 Silver Watch	22/-/-
2 Dozen China Cups & 2 Dozen Plates	7/12/-
2 Tea pots, 3 Large Platters, 2 small D^O	3/6/-

(...continued next page...)

---

[81] Peter Johnson to Sir William Johnson, April 21, 1774, *SWJP,* XIII, pp. 635–36; Peter Johnson to Sir William Johnson, April 30, 1774, *SWJP,* VIII, p. 1139.

[82] Guzzardo, p. 289.

[83] List prepared at Niagara, April 28, 1778, of effects and possessions left behind in 1777, quoted in Guldenzopf, pp. 204–05.

(Wary Gon wa tsi ja yenni...continued)

New York Currency [£]
[pounds/shillings/pence]

2 Basons & 2 Mugs	1/8/-
2 Large Pots, 6 Milk Pots, 4 Large D^O	4/2/-
1 Dozen Knives & Forks & 2 Brass Candlesticks	1/10/-
1 Pair Tongs & Shovel, 2 Common D^O	2/-/-
7 Smoothing Irons, 1 Gridiron & 1 Toaster	2/18/-
1 Tea Kettle, 1 Skillet, 2 Japan'd Candlesticks	2/-/-
12 Black Chairs, 3 Large Bowls & 12 Wine Glasses	5/4/-
2 Decanters, 12 Dozen Bottles & 4 Wooden Bowls	6/-/-
4 Large Canisters, 4 Small D^O	5/-/-
1 Fine Wagon & 1 Chaise & Geers [trappings]	50/-/-
1 Batteaux, 3 Side Saddles, 1 Mens Saddle	66/-/-
2 Large Brass Locks	2/-/-
Corn [grain] of all sorts	200/-/-
47 # Nails	2/7/-
2 Pair Green Velvet Leggens, 1 Black Velvet Blanket	10/-/-
1 Piece Chintz & 1 Piece Silk for Gowns	13/-/-
2 Scarlet Cloaks & 2 Black Silk D^O	18/-/-
4 Long Gowns, a White French Quilt & 1 Satten D^O	17/-/-
2 1/2 Dozen Cotton Stockings, 4 Pair Silk D^O	10/-/-
6 White Handkerfs, 2 Red Silk D & 3 Blue D^O	4/14/-
3 Check D^O, 6 Muslin Aprons, 3 Black D^O	7/16/-
3 Round Hats, 3 Bonnets, 2 Round D^O	11/8/-
2 Pair Silver Buckles, 200 Silver Broaches	13/4/-
300 Silver Crosses, 1 Large Looking Glass	18/-/-
2 Dwelling Houses & a Barn	400/-/-
2 Small D^O	16/-/-
3 Silk Waistcoats, 2 Pair Naukeen Breeches	12/-/-
3 White D^O, 2 Coats & Laced Hat, 4 Silk Short Gowns	21/-/-
1/2 Piece Fine Linen, 4 Pair Silk Gloves	6/16/-
2 Pair Womens Stockings, 3 Pair Cloth Shoes	1/12/-
3 Pair Leather Shoes	-/16/-
1 Violin & Set of Music Books & 1 Picture	16/-/-
3 Blankets, Red on One Side & Blue on the Other	12/-/-
1 Black Superfine Blanket & 1 Green D^O with Ribbons	8/-/-
2 Superfine D^O, 1 Blue & 1 Black with Ribbons	8/-/-

[Total] 1206/13/4

Household goods such as trunks, blankets, sheets, fine ceramics, utility ceramics, tableware and kitchen items were listed first along with cash. Following this were transportation items: a wagon, a chaise, a bateau and saddles. After an unspecified amount of corn (in 18th-century British usage this meant grain of any sort), valued at £200, were items of clothing, of both Indian and European style, items of adornment such as buckles, broaches and crosses (probably intended as gifts or trade items), shoes and a violin (probably Peter's). Molly Brant also noted that the Rebels had taken all of the "Deeds of writings" in her possession. The four dwelling houses and the barn included her mother's house complex, where Joseph Brant had been living and which came to Molly by right of matrilineal descent.

Peter Warren Johnson, son of Molly Brant and Sir William Johnson; artist unknown. *Courtesy, Metropolitan Toronto Library Board (T15018).*

Chapter Three
CANAJOHARIE AND CAYUGA

In his will, Sir William Johnson recognized his "natural" children by Molly Brant as "her" children. She came from a society based on matrilineal and matrilocal descent. Following these kinship practices, she left Johnson Hall in 1774 after Sir William's death and took all of their children back to her native village of Canajoharie. There they stayed for three years. Many years later, one of her daughters (probably Margaret Farley who moved to England in 1831) recalled that during their time at Canajoharie, her older sisters were sent to school in Schenectady.[84]

Peter returned from Philadelphia after his father's death and joined the British Indian Department under the command of Guy Johnson. Stationed near Montreal after the outbreak of the American Revolution in 1775, he saw action when Rebel forces marched into Canada that fall. When a detachment led by Ethan Allen made an unsuccessful premature strike against Montreal, Peter was the officer who accepted Allen's surrender outside the gates of the city in September.[85] This action came to the attention of New York colonial governor Tryon, who wrote to the Earl of Dartmouth that "the Indians have chosen Peter Johnson, the natural son of Sr. Wm. Johnson (by an Indian Woman) to be their Chief. He is intrepid and active, and took with his own hand Eathan Allen in a barn, after his detachment was routed near Montreal. The Indian Department demands all possible attention and a Commission of General to Peter would be politic."[86] In Ethan Allen's own account, published in 1779, he did not recognize the officer as an Indian although he described the manner and dress of the Indians who were there.[87] Peter Johnson must therefore have been dressed in British military clothing. In 1776, Peter went to England as part of a Loyalist delegation consisting partly of other members of his family: Sir John Johnson, Daniel Claus, Guy Johnson and Joseph Brant. Interestingly, Ethan Allen was a prisoner aboard that same vessel, and although he recognized Guy Johnson and Daniel Claus (Claus was the only

---

[84] "Testimony of a Child of Molly Brant," March 15, 1841, transcribed by Milton Hamilton, Albany Institute of History and Art, *Hamilton Papers,* Box 2, Folder 12.

[85] Col. Guy Johnson to the Earl of Dartmouth, Oct. 12, 1775, *DRCHSNY,* VIII, p. 637.

[86] Gov. William Tryon to the Earl of Dartmouth, Feb. 8, 1776, *Ibid,* p. 663.

[87] Ethan Allen, *The Narrative of Colonel Ethan Allen, 1779* (New York: 1961), pp. 20–22.

Reverend Samuel Kirkland. *Courtesy, Hamilton College, Clinton, New York.*

one who did not torment him), he did not mention the young officer who had captured him.

Molly Brant's political life also took on a new intensity with the beginning of revolution in 1775. The Johnsons and her brother Joseph were immediately involved in the Loyalist cause. No doubt her tendencies already were the same as theirs. However, she stayed in Canajoharie as long as possible, probably hoping all would be settled quickly. There, Molly and family became something of an attraction for travelers coming through the area. In August 1775, Tench Tilghman, secretary for an Indian commission appointed by the revolutionary Congress, stopped in Canajoharie to encourage the sachems to attend a conference at German Flatts. There he observed Molly Brant, whom he described as "fallen from her high Estate. She lived with Sr William for 20 years and was treated with as much attention as if she had been his wife .... she was of great use to Sr William in his Treaties with those people. He knew that Women govern the Politics of savages as well the refined part of the World." Tilghman added that Sir William left her "some money, upon which she carries on a small Trade, consisting chiefly, I believe in Rum which she sells to the Indians."[88]

Although Tilghman may have been repeating unfounded gossip, it is possible that Brant was selling rum to supplement her income. Sir William had arranged for her to inherit £1,200 from his estate, but how much of this she actually received remains unknown. Some of the money may have been invested in a store already being run by her brother Joseph, or she may have been participating in trade in a small way by herself. [89] Her Loyalist claim included a large number of silver broaches and silver crosses which could have been trade items or might have been used mostly as gifts.

The next day, when the Indians arrived at German Flatts for the conference with the Americans, Tilghman noted Molly Brant among them. "She saluted us with an air of ease and politeness, she was dressed after the Indian Manner, but her linen and other Cloathes the finest of their kind," he wrote. Tilghman added that when "... one of the Company that had known her before told her she looked thin and asked her if she had been sick, she said sickness had not reduced her, but that it was the Remembrance of a Loss that could never be made up to her, meaning the death of Sr. William. Upon seeing Mr. Kirkland an Oneida Missionary, she taxed him with neglect in passing by her House without calling to see her. She said there was a time when she had friends enough, but remarked with sensible emotion that the unfortunate and the poor were always neglected."[90]

Perhaps Brant had always acted this assertively, or perhaps Sir William's death had changed her. For whatever reason, she moved into the

---

[88] Harrison, p. 83.

[89] Kelsay, p. 117.

[90] Harrison, p. 87.

company of these authoritative white men with confidence. She responded emotionally to their queries. She charged one of their number with neglect. She certainly was not loath to express herself. The forceful missionary Samuel Kirkland did not intimidate her. He had stayed for a month at a time at Johnson Hall, and she had good reason to expect some acknowledgment of her former hospitality.

Tilghman went on to add a sentence that forecast her future: "The Indians pay her great respect and I am afraid her influence will give us some trouble, for we are informed that she is working strongly to prevent the meeting at Albany, being intirely in the Interests of Guy Johnson." Upon Sir William's death, Guy had become the Superintendent of Indian Affairs for the Northern District and had fled to Canada the previous June. He was a key player in the contest between the British and Americans to enlist the assistance, or at least the neutrality, of the Iroquois. Obviously, Molly Brant had a part to play in this struggle.

Sir John Johnson fled to Canada in 1776, leaving Johnson Hall in the hands of American troops. The officer in charge, Captain Joseph Bloomfield of New Jersey, kept a journal of events. After marching from Johnstown in June 1776, he passed Canajoharie, where "in this place lives Miss Molly (the noted Indian Squagh kept by Sir Wm. Johnson) & her Eight Children & who were all well provided for by the Vigorous old Baronet before his Death."[91] Molly Brant clearly was a well-known figure; even a military man from another colony was aware of the exact number of children she and Sir William had together. Eight days later, Bloomfield again called "at the house of Miss Molly ... & who by the generosity of her Paramour Sr. Wm. Johnson has every thing convenient around her & lives more in the English taste than any of her Tribe. She is now about 50 & has the remains of a Very likely Person."[92] Bloomfield was wrong; Brant was actually about forty years old. His account confirms, however, that she was living in a European-style house surrounded by goods she later listed in her Loyalist claim: fine ceramics, silver, twelve black chairs and other items. A month later, on July 14, Bloomfield "got a Pair of Elegant Leggins made in the Indian Fashion by Miss Molly & her Daughters .... Had the Pleasure of seeing the Young Ladys, one is Very handsome, both were richly dressed agreable to the Indian-Fashion."[93] Bloomfield may have ordered the leggings on his previous visit.

Not everyone, evidently, could get to see Molly's daughters. Another member of Bloomfield's party, Ebenezer Elmer, reported that on June 27 when he stopped to visit Sir William Johnson's "squaw" in hopes of meeting the daughters whom he identified as "the Miss Johnsons," he was told that "they were not up." He did see and converse with "the old squaw lady who

---

[91] Journal of Joseph Bloomfield, June 9, 1776, Lender and Martin, p. 61.

[92] June 17, 1776, *Ibid,* p. 63.

[93] July 14, 1776, *Ibid,* p. 72.

appeared kind."[94] This may either have been Molly Brant or her mother Margaret.

Brant and her children were finally forced to leave Canajoharie after the Battle of Oriskany, fought on August 6, 1777, when the Americans learned she had sent information to the British about their troop movements.[95] The bloody battle was fought near an Oneida settlement, and some of them, who were siding with the Americans, were burned out. Claus reported "this the rebel Oneidas ... revenged upon Joseph's Sister and her family (living in the Upper Mohawk Town) ... robbing them of cash, cloaths, cattle &c. and driving them from their home."[96] Molly's child testified later that they also were threatened by "persons who would remove [them] from Canajoharie to Albany." One night, men claiming to be looking for Joseph Brant searched the house. "I was in one of the beds of which they drew back the Curtains, & seeing only Children in it, they declined ferther Search - & withdrew. I perfectly remember my alarm." A few nights later, after a similar experience, "my Mother then determined to leave the Country as she found her residence ... no longer Safe. She left her House with reluctance & with a Sore heart taking her Children Seven in Number two black men Servants & two female Servants." The account concludes with a description of their hardships while traveling through the wilderness to Canada.[97] Daniel Claus, however, wrote that Brant and her children "fled to Onondaga the Council place of the 6 Nations, laying her grievances before that body. The Six Nations with whom she always had a great sway ... I understand ... have decreed to render her satisfaction by committing hostilities upon that tribe of Oneida rebels that committed the outrage."[98]

It is more likely that Molly Brant fled her home as a result of threats from the local Committee of Safety, and that the Oneida did their damage after her departure. In April 1778 Jelles Fonda, on behalf of the American Commissioners of Indian Affairs, visited Canajoharie and took affidavits documenting the plundering. He blamed the affair on former County Chairman Peter S. Dygart. "There has been a great deal of goods taken from Miss Mary Brant, formerly Sir Williams Miss and that family ... Dygart, and Hanyerey an [Oneida] Indian has Divided, Sixty half Johanneses, two Quarts full of Silver, Several Gold Rings, Eight pair silver Buckels; a Large Quanty of Silver Broaches, Together with several silk Gowns, which has

---

[94] Ebenezer Elmer, "Journal Kept During and Expedition to Canada in 1776," *New Jersey Historical Society Proceedings,* II (1847), p. 132.

[95] Claus to William Knox, Oct. 16, 1777, *DRCHSNY,* VIII, p. 721.

[96] Claus to Knox, Nov. 6, 1777, *Ibid,* p. 725.

[97] Testimony of a Child of Molly Brant's, March 15, 1841, *Hamilton Papers,* Box 2, Folder 12.

[98] Claus to Knox, Nov. 6, 1777, *DRCHSNY,* VIII, p. 725.

Guy Carleton. *Courtesy, National Archives of Canada, Ottawa.*

been seen by George Harkermer on the aforesaid Peter S. Dygarts Daughter."[99] The range and extent of the goods documented in this account correlate with Brant's Loyalist claim.

Molly Brant abandoned much of her wealth when she was forced to leave Canajoharie. She had stayed longer than other Johnson family members, probably to protect the inheritance promised to her and her children in Sir William's will. Throughout the war, she continued to plan for a return home. On June 23, 1778, for example, Molly wrote that she maintained "hope the Time is very near, when we shall all return to our habitations on the Mohawk River."[100]

The Battle of Oriskany drew attention to the beginnings of open warfare in the west. On August 19, 1777 John Adams, writing from Philadelphia to his wife Abigail, reported that "in the Northern Department they begin to fight. The Family of Johnson, the black part of it as well as the white, are pretty well thinned. Rascals! they deserve Extermination."[101] William of Canajoharie, one of the sons Sir William recognized in his will, was reported killed at Oriskany, along with many other Indians. He probably was of the "black part" to which Adams referred. Feelings about the foe ran deep on both sides during the American Revolution; this was a civil war as much as a war for "liberty."

The Iroquois were considered by both sides to be important components in the conflict. Governor Tryon wrote that:

> *... to fix and retain the Indians, by very liberal presents &*
> *encouragement will be of the highest importance to the*
> *King's service at this Crisis ... the Indian Nations will make*
> *a powerfull diversion on the Borders of the Lake ... cut off*
> *all Parties going to reinforce the enemy, and probably seize*
> *all the Vessels, Battaus, and Row Gallys before they are*
> *liberated from the ice, and then join General Carlton in*
> *Canada, or come down to Albany as occasion may require*
> *.... This, My Lord, is the Plan of Operations for the Indians*
> *and I expect it will be executed and succeed.*[102]

The Americans, having enlisted the assistance of the Oneida, hoped the rest of the Iroquois would at least stay neutral. Many did not. Various Iroquois forces fought on the side of the British, thereby fracturing the unity of their historic confederation.

---

[99] Jelles Fonda to the Board of Commissioners of Indian Affairs, April 21, 1778, Maryly B. Penrose (ed.), *Indian Affairs Papers* (Franklin Park, NJ: 1981), p. 134.

[100] Molly Brant to Daniel Claus, June 23, 1778, *Claus Papers,* MG19, F1, 2:29, transcribed by Wanda Burch.

[101] John Adams to Abigail Adams, August 19, 1777, L.H. Butterfield (ed.), *Adams Family Correspondence* (2 vols., New York: 1965), II, p. 320.

[102] Gov. William Tryon to the Earl of Dartmouth, Feb, 8, 1776, *DRCHSNY,* VIII, p. 664. This is the same letter in which Tryon suggested making Peter Johnson a general (see earlier reference, p. 41, n. 86).

Sir William Johnson, by Matthew Pratt. *Courtesy, New York State Office of Parks, Recreation and Historic Preservation; Johnson Hall State Historic Site.*

Brant and her family lived for a short time with relatives among the Cayuga, where she "fixed herself & family at the principals Chiefs house." She told Claus that after Burgoyne's defeat in the fall of 1777 she found the Iroquois "... in general very fickle & unstable, and even the head Man of the Senecas ... with whom she had a pointed Conversation in publick Council at Canadasegey [an Indian town located at present day Geneva in western New York] reminding him of the former great Friendship & Attachment which subsisted between him and the late Sr. Wm Johnson, whose Memory she never mentions but with Tears in her Eyes, which affects Indians greatly and to whom continued she, he so often declared & promised to live and die a firm Friend & Ally to the King of England and his Friends, with other striking arguments and Reasonings, which had such an Effect upon that Chief and the rest of the 5 Nations present, that they promised her faithfully to stick up strictly to the Engagements to her late worthy Friend and for his & her sake espouse the Kings Cause vigorously and speadily avenge her Wrongs & Injuries, for she is in every Respect considered & esteemed by them as Sr. Wms Relict, and one word from her is more taken Notice of by the five Nations than a thousand. from any white Man without Exception."[103]

Molly Brant was deeply committed to the British cause. She had become a significant political force and did not hesitate to use her influence. Her status as Sir William's widow enhanced the power she already had developed while participating in Indian affairs at Johnson Hall.

---

[103] Claus to Gov. Frederick Haldimand, Aug. 30, 1779, *Haldimand Papers,* Add. MSS 21774, pp. 57–58. See also Claus to Haldimand, Aug. 30, 1779, *Claus Papers,* MG19, F1, 2:131–33. These are two different letters, each often quoted. Written on the same day, the version used here was sent to Haldimand; the other was a draft kept by Claus.

Lieutenant-Colonel John Butler. *Courtesy, Niagara Historical Society, Niagara-on-the-Lake, Ontario.*

Chapter Four
FORT NIAGARA

British authorities soon recognized that the power held by Molly Brant could be used in their war effort. Major John Butler, later lieutenant-colonel, successfully urged her to come to Niagara where both Indian and British forces were gathering. She arrived there in late 1777. Fort Niagara, located on Lake Ontario at the mouth of the Niagara River, dominated the waterway to the west. The fort had been captured in 1759 from the French, by British forces under the command of Sir William Johnson. As a strong fortress, it was a natural headquarters for the British and a frequent base of operations for their Indian allies. There Butler had begun to organize his Corps of Rangers that would use Fort Niagara "as a base from which to scourge the American frontiers between 1777 and 1783."[104]

John Butler had been a trader, officer of the Indian Department, and an old ally from the Mohawk Valley. He had been appointed by Sir William as one of the guardians for Molly Brant's children. Therefore, he knew her and was well aware of her influence with the Iroquois. At a conference he held at Niagara in 1776, Butler had tried to impress them with the readiness of the British for war: "[we] are well provided with Arms, Ammunition & every thing necessary, whilst the Americans are destitute of all these they have not one pound of powder, where we have a thousand, nor a pound of Lead where we have ten thousand, nor do they know how to fight." He then added, "take up the Hatchet & your old Men & Women, your Wives & Children shall be well taken care of. They may live in our Forts–We will both feed and cloathe them."[105] Most of the Iroquois present were not yet ready to join either side, but, in the end, Butler's invitation would prevail with many of them.

It is uncertain exactly where Molly Brant and her family resided while at Fort Niagara. An Oneida Indian reported, in December 1780, that only the British lived within the walls; Loyalists were on the other side of the river in barracks, and the Indians were living around the fort.[106] It has been

---

[104] Brian Leigh Dunnigan, *Siege - 1759: The Campaign Against Niagara* (Youngstown, NY: 1996), p. 125; a profusely illustrated, concise study of the 1759 siege and Sir William Johnson's part in it.

[105] Speech given by John Butler at an Indian conference at Fort Niagara, June 4, 1776, quoted in Gregory Schaaf, *Wampum Belts & Peace Trees: George Morgan, Native American and Revolutionary Diplomacy* (Golden, CO: 1990), p. 106.

[106] Interview of Jacob Reid, Oneida, by Col. Weissenfels, Dec. 9, 1780, *Public Papers of George Clinton, First Governor of New York, 1777–1795–1801–1804* (10 vols.; Albany: 1899-1914), VI, p. 482.

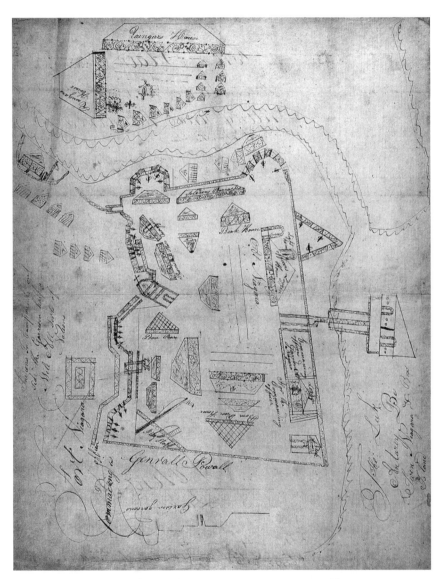

Plan of Fort Niagara, c. 1780-81, by John Luke. Written on the plan is the notation "Indians In Campments out Side The Garrison half a Mile…All Sorts of Nations."
Courtesy, American Antiquarian Society.

reported that Molly Brant lived in a house built there for her by General Haldimand, commander of the British forces in Canada.[107]

Her presence at Niagara proved useful. From January to June 1779, six conferences were held at Fort Niagara involving almost 3,000 Indians.[108] As Claus explained, "she having been their Confidant in every Matter of Importance & was consulted thereupon, and prevented many an unbecoming & extravagant proposal to the Commanding Officer at Niagara."[109] In an earlier draft of this letter, Claus also wrote that "she prevented many at mischief & much more so than in her Bror Joseph whose present Zeal & Activity occasioned rather Envy & Jealousy."[110]

Utilizing Niagara as a base, Molly Brant traveled to Montreal where she placed some of the children in school. When Claus sent her a small trunk by way of merchants Taylor and Duffin, they were not able to give it to her because she was "away visiting the Indian towns." They reported a successful delivery in October 1778 of both the trunk and £25 Halifax currency from General Haldimand, for which "she is mightily pleased with his Excellcy's notice of her." Brant told Taylor that "if it were not for the Service She thinks She can be of here: in advising & conversing with the Indians: She wou'd go down to Canada with her Family. She desires Mr. Taylor to inform you [Claus] the Manner She lives here is pretty expensive to her: being oblidged to keep, in a manner, open house for all those Indians that have any weight in the 6 Nations confederacy." Recognizing her worth, Taylor and Duffin "told her we will not see her in want."[111] This is particularly telling, because in the same letter they informed Claus that although Joseph Brant desperately needed supplies for his troops, they would provide him with only "such things as they cannot do without untill we hear farther from you." Apparently, however, the two merchants had been instructed to support Molly in the work she was doing. Further example of her vital role was illustrated a month later when Claus asked Molly "to communicate ... Intelligence to her Brother & the Chiefs of the 6 Nations & with my Salutation and Request to persavere faithful to their antient Friend and Ally the Great King of England."[112] Thus, at Niagara as elsewhere, Molly Brant was acting as a conduit for the encouragement and information that was flowing between the British government and the

---

[107] Jean Johnston, "Molly Brant: Mohawk Matron," *Ontario History,* LVI, No. 2 (June 1964), p. 117, citing the *Haldimand Papers,* B114 MG21, p. 42.

[108] Kelsay, p. 236.

[109] Claus to Haldimand, Aug. 30, 1779, *Haldimand Papers,* Add. MSS 21774, pp. 57–58.

[110] Draft of a letter from Claus to Haldimand (not sent), Aug. 30, 1779, *Claus Papers,* MG19, F1, 2:131–33, transcribed by Wanda Burch.

[111] Taylor and Duffin to Daniel Claus, Oct. 26, 1778, Penrose, pp. 167–68.

[112] Daniel Claus to Haldimand, Nov. 5, 1778, *Ibid,* p. 169.

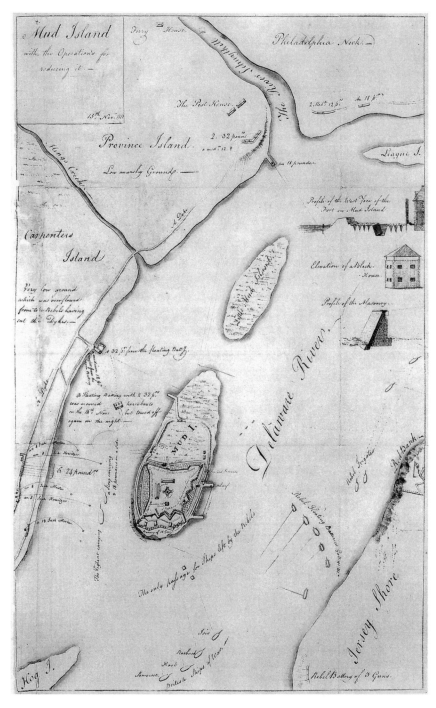

Drawing of the battle plan used by British forces to reduce Fort Mifflin on Mud Island, in November 1777. *Courtesy, Huntington Library, San Marino, California.*

Iroquois. Meanwhile, she was living in a crowded, predominantly male environment separated from those children at school in Montreal and from her son, Peter. Her political activities had become more important than her domestic ones.

During his time in England, Peter had successfully solicited a commission as ensign in the regular army.[113] Reportedly returning to America in 1776, Peter had "gone with Howe to Philadelphia and had lost his life at Mud Island" in 1777.[114] Fort Mifflin, the "Mud Island" fortification, was one of the American Delaware River strongholds below Philadelphia and was taken by the British in November. No record has been found of his mother's reaction to the news of his death. However, in November 1778 Molly expressed sorrow to a merchant at Fort Niagara, telling him she "is under a great concern at the loss of her two Sons, being dear to her — were they still alive, she thinks one of them might be with her sometimes."[115] The other "son" was William of Canajoharie who erroneously was reported killed at Oriskany just three months before the fighting at Mud Island.

The strain of family and material losses, coupled with her many duties at Niagara, may have overwhelmed Molly Brant at this point. An account of life at Niagara, published in 1831 and based on the recollections of Revolutionary War veterans, indicates that she became hostile to Lieutenant Colonel-William Stacey, an American captive. "She resorted to the Indian method of dreaming. She informed Col. Butler that she dreamed she had the Yankee's head, and that she and the Indians were kicking it about the fort .... she dreamed a second time that she had the Yankee's head, with his hat on, and she and the Indians were kicking it about the fort for a football .... Col. Butler then told her, decidedly, that Col. Stacia should not be given up to the Indians."[116] Lieutenant-Colonel Stacey, of Colonel Ichabod Alden's Massachusetts Regiment, had been captured at Cherry

---

[113] The *Army List* for 1777 carries the one "P. Johnston" as ensign in the 26th Regiment of Foot. The name is not in the list for 1778. *Army List* (London, 1777), p. 80. The 26th had been stationed in northern New York and Canada at the outbreak of the war where Peter and his patrons were likely to have had contact with its officers. The regiment, which had been captured by the Rebels during the 1775 Canadian campaign but later exchanged and reconstituted, was sent to reinforce Howe's army during the later stages of the 1777 Philadelphia campaign. Philip R. N. Katcher, *Encyclopedia of British, Provincial and German Army Units, 1775-1783* (Harrisburg, PA: 1973), p. 42.

[114] Kelsay, pp. 174, 272; Peter also was reported to have lost his life at the Battle of Long Island. *SWJP*, XII, p. 966n; *SWJP*, XIII, p. 1025n. Evidence is inconclusive. The 26th Regiment of Foot did not participate in the Battle of Long Island, but it was in the closing stages of the Philadelphia campaign which included the attacks on the Mud Island Fort (Fort Mifflin). Katcher, p. 42.

[115] Johnston, "Molly Brant: Mohawk Matron," p. 118; Jean Johnston, "Molly Brant," in her *Wilderness Women: Canada's Forgotten History* (Toronto: 1973), p. 99.

[116] William W. Campbell, *Annals of Tryon County; Or, the Border Wars of New-York, During the Revolution* (New York: 1831), p. 182. It should be noted that the 'Indian method of dreaming' was and is an important Iroquois belief. Dreams represent wishes that, for the health of the dreamer, should be fulfilled. Both Iroquois and whites tried to do this when possible.

View of Fort Niagara, c. 1785, by James Peachey. *Courtesy, William L. Clements Library.*

View of Fort Niagara (from the south), c. 1784-85, by an English artist (probably James Peachey) showing crowded housing below the Fort, on the Niagara River. *Courtesy, William L. Clements Library.*

Valley in November 1778. While stationed there at Fort Alden, Stacey had participated in raids against Joseph Brant's party and had served on a court of inquiry against those captured.[117] Molly may have resented this or possibly had other words with Stacey. For whatever reason, she may have been demanding revenge. In any event, the dream was not fulfilled. Joseph Brant's biographer, Isabel Kelsay, points out that the commandant of Fort Niagara, Lieutenant-Colonel Mason Bolton, "actually did send this prisoner down to Montreal for fear of what the Indians might do to him. His action lends some credence to the story."[118]

By June 1779, Fort Niagara had become so crowded that the commandant suggested that Molly Brant and her family be transferred to Montreal.[119] In reality, this request might have been made because of Brant's difficult behavior or because Bolton was concerned that conditions at Niagara made it impossible for her to receive the best treatment. General Frederick Haldimand, commander of the British forces in Canada, responded positively, and on July 16, Colonel Bolton wrote that "Miss Molly & Family have accepted your Excellency's Invitation and will leave this place to–morrow."[120] Upon Daniel Claus' return to Montreal, in August, Brant visited him and recounted her adventures since the fall of 1777. He reported that she was unhappy about leaving Niagara because she had "to leave her old Mother & other Indn Relations & friends behind .... besides her Absence would be regretted by the generality of the five Nations .... She seems not at all reconciled to this Place & Country; having two grown Daughters with her whom she would willingly see appear decent which is not in her power to do, and I am apprehensive her staying here would be more expensive than at Niagara, she being so near the Fountain head."[121]

---

[117] Maj. Daniel Whiting to Gen. Hand, Nov. 13, 1778, *Public Papers of George Clinton,* IV, p. 286; Abraham Ten Broeck to George Clinton, Nov. 17, 1778, *Ibid.,* p. 292; Clinton to Col. Philip van Cortlandt, Nov. 18, 1778, *Ibid.,* p 293; Ichabod Alden to Gen. Stark, Aug. 26, 1778, *Public Papers of George Clinton,* V, p. 416; Court of Inquiry, Sept. 10, 1778, *Ibid.,* p. 417.

[118] Kelsay, p. 686, n2.

[119] Haldimand to Lt.-Col. John Butler, June 7, 1779, *Haldimand Papers,* Add. MSS 21764, p. 18.

[120] Gundy, p. 102.

[121] Claus to Haldimand, Aug. 30, 1779, *Haldimand Papers,* Add. MSS 21774, pp. 57–58.

General Frederick Haldimand. *Courtesy, National Archives of Canada, Ottawa (C3221).*

Chapter Five
CARLETON ISLAND

Molly Brant did not stay in Montreal. In the late summer of 1779 an American military force under generals John Sullivan and James Clinton marched into the western Iroquois country and began destroying villages and crops in an effort to end Six Nations participation in the war. As American general Philip Schuyler explained to George Washington, one of the purposes of the campaign was to force the Seneca to "move to Niagara and continue there until next spring at least, and being there, so distant from our frontiers without any Intermediate place to procure subsistance, no considerable body will venture to molest us, and before they can reestablish themselves in their towns, events will probably arise which will place them wholly in our power."[122] Molly Brant's immediate response was a desire to return to Niagara, as she believed "... her Staying away at this critical Time, may prove very injurious to her character hereafter, being at the head of a Society of six Natn Matrons, who have a great deal to say among the young Men in particular in time of War, ... for if she was to forsake them now, they might impute it to Fear, and that she forsaw or knew of an impending Danger over the Confederacy which she kept concealed and went out of the way to avoid it, wch Reflection would be insupportable to her."[123]

Haldimand agreed that "If she thinks her presence necessary above, she must be suffered to depart – Colonel Johnson will of course provide for her Journey, and give her whatever Presents may be necessary."[124] To Guy Johnson, he added "I have acquainted Colonel Claus that Miss Molly is to act as she thinks best, whether in remaining in this Province, or Returning to the Seneca Country:– and that you or Col: Claus will give her Such Presents as you may think necessary, and if she goes, provide for her Journey as it Seems to be a Political one."[125] Johnson agreed that "she will be of great use to the Kings Service at this time."[126] During this period of

---

[122] Gen. Philip Schuyler to Gen. George Washington, March 1, 1779, Penrose, pp. 187–88.

[123] Claus to Haldimand, Sept. 6, 1779, *Haldimand Papers,* Add. MSS 21174, p. 63.

[124] Haldimand to Claus, Sept. 9, 1779, *Ibid,* p. 65.

[125] Haldimand to Guy Johnson, Sept. 9, 1779, *Haldimand Papers,* Add. MSS 21767, p. 29.

[126] Guy Johnson to Haldimand, Sept. 19, 1779, *Ibid,* p. 31.

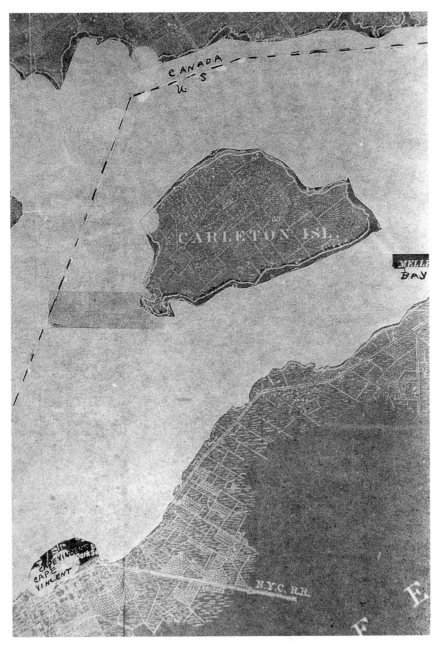

Carleton Island (in the present day town of Cape Vincent, New York). From a modified map of Jefferson County, c. 1978. *Courtesy, New York State Office of Parks, Recreation and Historic Preservation; Bureau of Field Services.*

crisis, the British establishment was well aware of Molly Brant's political role and how useful she could be. Haldimand justified his decision in a letter to Lord George Germain, Secretary of State for the Colonies, written in September 1779. After describing Joseph Brant's importance, he reported that Molly "might be of use in encouraging the Indians to Preserve their Fidelity .... the Care of this Woman will necessarily be attended with Some Expense to Government, but whatever may be done for her, is Due to the Memory of Sir Willm Johnson, to Her Services, and will be a handsome Mark of attention to Joseph."[127] Brant, however, was also concerned about her family. Haldimand had suggested to both Claus and Guy Johnson that she leave her children at school.[128] Guy Johnson replied that he would "furnish her in the manner you are pleased to mention, but her anxiety to have her Children with her seems insurmountable, however I shall manage about it in the best manner in my power."[129] As a result, Molly accompanied a group of Mohawk to Carleton Island, leaving her two youngest girls with Daniel Claus "to send to School one is 10. the other 8. year old."[130] The rest of the family apparently went with her.

Carleton Island, at the head of the St. Lawrence River, was the location of a British post situated to protect the waterway between Montreal and the Great Lakes. The island is opposite present-day Alexandria Bay, New York. Here, however, the family was unable to get transport to Niagara. Brant's letter to Claus explaining their situation may have been written by her or dictated to an amanuensis. As one of her few extant letters, it captures her own words.

> *Carleton Island 5th. October 1779*
>
> Sir
>
> *We arrived here the 29th. last month after Tedious and dissagreable Voyage; where we remain and by all Appearance may for the winter I have rote to Colo. Butler and my brother Acquainting them of my Situation, desireing there advice, as I was left no Direction Concerning my self or family, Only when a Vessel Arraived [sic], I Could get a passage to Niagara — I have been promised by Colo. Johnson at Montreal that I Should hear from the Gen'l. and have his directions in order to be provided at whatever place my little services should be wanted which you know I am always ready to do, Should you think proper to speak*

---

[127] Haldimand to Lord George Germain, Sept. 13, 1779, *Haldimand Papers,* Add. MSS 21714, p. 42.

[128] Haldimand to Guy Johnson, Sept. 9, 1779, *Haldimand Papers,* Add. MSS 21767, p. 29; Haldimand to Daniel Claus, Sept. 9, 1779, *Haldimand Papers,* Add. MSS 21174, p. 65.

[129] Guy Johnson to Haldimand, Sept. 19, 1779, *Haldimand Papers,* Add. MSS 21767, p. 31.

[130] Claus to Haldimand, Sept. 13, 1779, *Haldimand Papers,* Add. MSS 21774, p. 279.

Portrait by Benjamin West, believed to be Guy Johnson, nephew of Sir William Johnson and his successor as Indian Commissioner. *Courtesy, National Gallery of Art, Washington; Andrew W. Mellon Collection.*

to the Gen'l. on that head will be much Oblidged to you the
Indians are a Good dale dissatisfied on Acc't. of the Colo's.
hasty temper which I hope he will soon drop Otherwise it
may be Disadvantageous I need not tell you whatever is
promised or told them it Ought to be performed —

Those from Canada are much Dissatisfied on Account of
his taking more Notice of those that are suspected than
them that are known to be Loyal, I tell this only to you that
you Advise him On that head. Meantime beg leave to be
remembred to all Your family from Sir —

> *our*
> *wellwisher*
> *Mary Brant*

My Children Join in love to theire Sisters
Colo. Danl. Claus   Montreal [131]

"Colonel Johnson" was Guy, who was becoming more and more frustrated with his role as Superintendent of Indian Affairs. He may also have become frustrated with Brant and she with him. A month later he complained to Claus that he had heard that "Molly used to go to the Stores & take out everything she pleas'd & give to her particulars. She is certainly you know pretty large minded ... I fear that any Expense or Attention will fall short of her Desires tho' I wish to gratify them & many other things are said that I cannot now Explain."[132] Johnson probably referred to Brant's recent visit to Montreal where she apparently provisioned herself and her entourage generously from the general stores. Knowing that the facilities at Carleton Island were inadequate, he anticipated her need for better accommodations which he felt unable to provide. Although the action had nothing to do with Molly Brant, Guy Johnson was replaced by Sir John Johnson as Indian Commissioner shortly thereafter.

The British military response to the Clinton and Sullivan campaign was a failure. Hundreds of homeless Iroquois were left to winter on Carleton Island and at Fort Niagara. Molly Brant did what she could to maintain their fidelity to the British cause. By February 23, 1780, Captain Malcolm Fraser, in command there, wrote that Brant had "shewen her usual Zeal for Gov't. by her constant endeavours to maintain the Indians in His Majestys Interest."[133] On March 21, he added that "... the Chiefs were careful to keep their people sober and satisfied ... their uncommon good behaviour is in a great Measure to be ascribed to Miss Molly Brants Influence over them,

---

[131] Mary Brant to Claus, Oct. 5, 1779, *Claus Papers,* MG19, F1, 2:135–36, transcribed by Wanda Burch.

[132] Guy Johnson to Claus, Nov. 21, 1779, *Hamilton Papers,* Box 1, Folder 12, transcribed by M. Hamilton from the *Claus Papers.*

[133] Capt. Malcolm Fraser to Claus, Feb. 23, 1780, *Claus Papers,* MG19, F1, 2:177, transcribed by Wanda Burch.

Sir John Johnson, son of Sir William Johnson and Catherine Weissenberg. John succeeded to his father's baronetcy and followed Guy Johnson as Indian Super-intendent. *Courtesy, New York State Office of Parks, Recreation and Historic Preservation; Johnson Hall State Historic Site.*

which is far superior to that of all their Chiefs put together and she has in the course of the Winter done everything in Her power to maintain them strongly in the Kings Interest; and tho she is insatiable in her demands for her own family, yet I believe her residence here has been a considerable saving to Government, as she checkd the demands of others both for presents & provisions."[134]

While fulfilling her political role, Brant also worked to satisfy her domestic obligations. By June 21, 1780, with better quarters not yet available, she elected to go to Montreal to appeal directly to Haldimand. This caused much consternation. Fraser wrote from Carleton Island that "Joseph Brants' Sister Miss Molly left this place yesterday along with Colonel Butler much against my inclination as I have been informed she is gone to ask Your Excellency for favors & I have no Doubt but She will be unreasonable in her Demands – her family however is numerous, and not easily maintained in the decent footing on which she keeps them."[135] Claus, writing to John Johnson, reported "last Thursday arrived at my House Molly with her son George & her Attednt. Butler from Carleton Island ... [to] get something done for her ... to attain a certain Settlement upon her & children, three of whom become now soon marriageable, ... and she expects an answer by Saturday." Claus suggested that a regular allowance of £200 a year be awarded to her.[136] Between them, Claus and John Johnson persuaded Brant to leave the situation in their hands.

Meanwhile, Fraser, in his June 1780 letter to Haldimand, was sputtering;

> ... she will probably wish to change her place of Residence and may want to go to Niagara where she will be a very unwelcome Guest to Col. Bolton and most of the other principal people in that quarter, and if She be not humoured in all her demands for herself and her dependents (which are numerous) she may by the violence of her temper be led to creat Mischief. I therefore judge it would be better she remained where she was all winter or go down to Canada than live where the Mohawks or her other adherents are — In case Your Excellency would wish her to remain here it were good that some little box of a house were built for her as it would be more comfortable to her family than living in a Barrack Room.[137]

With such a large family, Molly Brant was justifiably unhappy with

---

[134] Fraser to Haldimand, March 21, 1780, *Haldimand Papers,* Add. MSS 21787, p. 116.

[135] Fraser to Haldimand, June 21, 1780, *Ibid.,* p. 150.

[136] Claus to John Johnson, June 26, 1780, *Hamilton Papers,* Box 1, Folder 12, transcribed by M. Hamilton from the Claus Papers.

[137] Fraser to Haldimand, June 21, 1780, *Haldimand Papers,* Add. MSS 21787, p. 150.

quartering as cramped and undignified as a barracks room; Fraser on his part was afraid of losing her assistance in handling the numerous Indians staying on the island. Haldimand reassured Fraser in July that Molly wished to stay at Carleton Island. He was ordered to build for her "a House as will lodge Her and Family comfortably, chuising a favorable Situation within a few hundred Yards of the Fort."[138] Fraser had indicated in his June 1780 letter that he had already "at my own expence made a tollerable good garden for her and I have contributed all in my power to have made her Situation as comfortable as possible – indeed she seems very well pleased with her treatment, and I have every reason to be satisfyed with her Conduct through the winter – and as I know herself and her family to be steadily attached to Government I wish them to be attended to."[139] Upon relinquishing command of the island to Major John Ross in 1781, Fraser reported that "I gave particular directions regarding Miss Molly's treatment, she had got into her new house, and seemed better satisfyed with her situation than I had ever known her before."[140] Molly had won.

Brant resided at Carleton Island for the remainder of the war. Her younger children continued to go to school in Montreal. On July 26, 1781, Claus wrote to Haldimand that:

> Ms. Mary Brant has been here for some days, and yesterday set off for Carleton Island again, taking away her Son George, and Susan & Mary two of her Daughters who were here at School near 2. years, Margaret an older Sister left this abt. a year ago; The Schoolmaster tells me that the girls sufficiently read & write English, and the Boy to my knowledge has greatly improved in that respect, and is so far advanced in cyphering that with a little care and Study he may easily require more of that Science than he will have occasion for, I have supplied him with necessary Books & Stationary, he is a promising Lad abt. 14 year old ... There are left at School two of Brant Johnson's Daughters, whose Mother is daily expected to take them away, the eldest a fine genius & great Arithmetician.[141]

Almost exactly a year later, on July 25, 1782, Claus wrote "Brant Johnsons two girls are lately gone to Niagara having finished their Learning after a 3. years stay at this place. A Boy and Girl of Mary Johnsons remain, but expect to be taken away shortly by their Mother."[142] In this note, Claus may

---

[138] Capt. Robert Matthews to Fraser, July 17, 1780, *Haldimand Papers,* Add. MSS 21788, p. 94.

[139] Fraser to Haldimand, June 21, 1780, *Haldimand Papers,* Add. MSS 21787, p. 150.

[140] Fraser to Haldimand, Jan. 1781, *Haldimand Papers,* Add. MSS 21787, p. 201.

[141] Claus to Haldimand, July 26, 1781, *Haldimand Papers,* Add. MSS 21774, p. 208.

[142] Claus to Haldimand, July 25, 1782, *Ibid.,* p. 279.

have called Molly Brant by the last name of Johnson, the only time that occurred in the known documentation, although the children all used the surname of Johnson. Brant Johnson's daughters, grandchildren of Sir William Johnson, were also being educated in the same school with their cousins.

In a "Return of Loyalists on Carleton Island" dated November 26, 1783, Molly Brant's household was listed under the category of "Indian Department."[143]

Names and Sexes	Age
Mrs. Mary Brant	47
Miss Elizabeth Johnson	20
Miss Margaret Johnson	16
Miss Magdalen Johnson	18
Miss Mary Johnson	12
Miss Susanah Johnson	11
Miss Nancy Johnson	10
William Lamb	13
Abraham Johnston, a negro	45
Juba Fundy a Negro woman	23
Jane Fundy a Negro Woman	20

This is the earliest document known to record Molly Brant's age and is the basis for her accepted birth date of 1736. Her daughters were all with her while son George had apparently gone back to school. Three slaves were present at Carleton Island, probably three of the four who had escaped with her from Canajoharie in 1777. The two female slaves were originally from Johnson Hall. Jane (Jenny) specifically was left to Brant in Johnson's will, along with one-quarter of his other slaves.[144] Jenny's sister, Juba, apparently was one of those. Molly, then, had managed to keep her household together, despite all the upsets and changes in their lives.

Present with them also was the thirteen-year-old captive, William Lamb, Jr. He and his father were taken captive by Joseph Brant and his men at Harpersfield, Delaware County, New York, in April 1780 when the boy was ten years old. They and thirteen others were collecting sap and making maple sugar, as well as scouting the countryside for Loyalists, when they were surprised. Although some of the party were killed, most were taken on a difficult wintry overland trip to Fort Niagara.[145] From

---

[143] Return of Loyalists on Carleton Island, Nov. 26, 1783, *Haldimand Papers,* Add. MSS 21787, p. 344.

[144] Will of Sir William Johnson, Jan. 27, 1774, *SWJP,* XII, p. 1070.

[145] Freegift Patchin, "Story of Revolutionary Days in Schoharie County, Captivity and Sufferings of General Freegift Patchin as Related by Himself," *St. Johnsville Enterprise,* Jan. 12-Feb. 16,1928. Based on interviews by Josiah Priest, c.1830.

Joseph Brant, by Gilbert Charles Stuart. This portrait, completed in London in 1786, was commissioned for Francis Rawdon, Earl of Moira. A slightly different variation of this, also painted (1786) for Rawdon, is in the collection of the British Museum. A third work (1786) was done by Stuart for Hugh Percy, 2nd Duke of Northumberland, and a close friend of Brant. *Courtesy, New York State Historical Association, Cooperstown, New York (N-199.61).*

there, the Lambs were transported to Carleton Island where Molly Brant probably saw the young prisoner whose family she might have known from the Mohawk Valley. She apparently made arrangements to keep him with her. William Lamb, Sr. spent time in prison at Chambly before returning home at the end of the war. Meanwhile, young Lamb probably served the Molly Brant household as servant and perhaps as companion to George Johnson who was close to the same age. According to one source, William Lamb, Jr. did not return home for eleven years![146] He unexpectedly showed up at his aunt's house in Schoharie in 1791 where his father came to bring him home. It is not known why young Lamb stayed away so long after hostilities ceased. It is very possible that Brant considered him adopted according to the Iroquois custom of replacing a lost family member with a captive. Lamb may, in fact, have been a substitute for her son Peter.[147]

While at Carleton Island, Molly Brant, successful in keeping her own household together and even adding another child to it, constantly worried about her brother Joseph. In April 1781, she wrote to Claus, "it touches me very sore to hear from Niagara how my younger Brother Joseph Brant was used the 6th of April, by being almost murdered by Col: Johnsons people, what adds to my grief and Vexation is, that being scarce returned safe from the rebel Country, he must be thus treated by these of the Kings people who always stay quietly at home & in the Fort, while my Brother Continually exposes his Life in going against the Enemy taking pris.rs [prisoners] as far as in his power." After urging that Haldimand intervene before the Iroquois become resentful, she added "it is hard for me to have an only Bror. whom I dearly love to see him thus treated, but what I am most concerned about is that it may affect the Kings Indn. Interest. The whole Matter is, that the Officers at Niagara are so haughty & proud, not knowing or considering that the Kings Interest is so nearly connected with that of the Indians."[148] The original letter was written in Mohawk, but only the English transcription is known to be extant.

---

[146] David Murray (ed.), *Delaware County, New York, History of the Century, 1797-1897* (Delhi, NY: 1898), p. 427.

[147] Eldon P Gundry, *William Lamb of Delaware County, New York, and His Descendants* (1957), p. 206. Lamb remained part of the Brant household but, according to the family geneology, also lived as servant to Sir John Johnson until he was twenty–one (Gundry 1957:206). Once back in Harpersfield, young Lamb married Martha Tharp, and they eventually relocated to Springport, Cayuga County, New York, where he died in 1854 at the age of 85. His will is on file at the County seat of Auburn. It is signed with an "X" so apparently William Lamb's years away did not include any schooling, and he lost what little literacy he might have had before his capture. In his will, he left generous inheritances to his nine children, an indication that he became very prosperous as well as long–lived. Lamb and his wife, two children, and his father–in–law, Joseph Tharp, are buried in the small Lamb cemetery located on Webb Road near Auburn. It is frustrating that he apparently left no written record of his years of captivity. The inventory of his household goods which once was attached to his will is missing from the County records. It would be interesting to know if his possessions included any Indian material.

[148] Mary Brant to Claus, April 12, 1781, *Haldimand Papers*, Add. MSS 21774, p. 180.

Present on Carleton Island with a small household was another Loyalist woman well known to the Iroquois, one Sarah McGinness. She had also been at Niagara. According to Daniel Claus, McGinness, née Kast, was born in the Mohawk Valley "next the Six Nation Country ... was from her childhood ... much loved by the 6 Nats. so far that they prevailed upon her parents to let her live among them, and adopted her as one of themselves, whereby she acquired the language perfectly."[149] Sarah Kast married Timothy McGinness (familiarly known as 'Teady' or 'Tedy Magin'), a captain in the Indian Department, and one of Sir William Johnson's close aides. She frequently assisted in Indian affairs. McGinness was killed at the Battle of Lake George when Sarah was forty–two years old; therefore, when the Revolutionary War broke out, she was sixty–two. Claus was very sympathetic about the deprivations the Kast/McGinness family suffered as Loyalists before escaping to Canada. However, he asked Sarah to go back into the Iroquois country carrying wampum belts and a few goods. She reluctantly agreed and went to a Cayuga village where the Iroquois gathered to hear her Loyalist message. While she was there, belts and messages arrived from American general Philip Schuyler with "a most exaggerated Acct. of Genl. Burgoynes Disaster with Invitations to the 6 Nations to join the Rebels." The Indians consulted with McGinness who, after giving her opinion and advice, "with an Authority and priviledge allowed Women of Consequence only among Indians, seized upon and cancelled the [Schuyler] belts, telling them that such bad News came from an evil spirit and must be buried under Ground which she would undertake to do, and in Reality carried her point that the Belts were carried no farther, tho they were to go among the Western Indians."[150]

Past experiences and more recent adventures would have given McGinness and Brant much to discuss. Brant had been living among the Cayuga while McGinness was there. Perhaps their paths had crossed. Whatever their relationship, Brant probably treated this much older woman with great respect. It seems probable that during the long winters on Carleton Island, and earlier at Niagara, the two women had many conversations together, in Mohawk. After the war, both moved to Cataraqui, on the northeast shore of Lake Ontario. McGinness died there in 1791 at the age of seventy–eight.[151]

---

[149] Claus to Haldimand, Nov. 5, 1778, Penrose, pp. 169–72.

[150] *Ibid.*

[151] H.C. Burleigh, *Deforests of Avesnes and Kast, McGinness*, published typescript ([N.p.:1977?]) in Special Collections, James A. Gibson Library, Brock University, St. Catharines, ON. The name of Timothy McGinness has appeared in various other works as *Teddy McGinnis* or *Teddy McGinness*. The spelling of *McGinness* has also appeared as *McGinnis*. Burleigh's work uses *McGinness* throughout, but inaccurately cites that spelling from a November 5, 1778 letter to Gen. Haldimand from Lt. Col. Daniel Claus (Burleigh, p. 9), and also, erroneously credits the letter to William Claus (Burleigh, p. 6). Further, the spellings used by Daniel Claus in the original handwritten letter are *Tedy M'Gennis, Mrs. M'Gennis,* and, *Mrs. M'Ginnis.* In a subsequent letter to Haldimand, on Nov. 19, 1778, Claus uses *Mrs. M'Kennis*

Life was not all drudgery on Carleton Island. In February 1780, Gilbert Tice, former Johnstown inn keeper, wrote to Claus that "Miss Molley and the Children are in Good Helth - and wee Pass our time Verey Agreabel Considering all things. wee have a Ball once a week-and Sevarel other things to Pass the time."[152] This remark followed his report that she had assisted him in explaining Claus's letter fully to the Indians. The work was not forgotten either.

Brant did not simply settle down on the island. In December 1780, Matilda Schieffelin, the wife of an Army officer, wrote from Navy Hall, across the river from Fort Niagara, to her father that:

> ... we were overtaken by Capt. Butler, son of the Colonel of that name .... When we had pitched our tent and seated ourselves by a good fire ... he joined us, bringing with him the famous Molly, formerly favorite Sultana to Sir William Johnson. I had the honor to sup with her in Captain Butler's Tent, on a haunch of Venison. She has a sensible countenance and much whiter than the generality of Indians, but her Father was white. She understands English but speaks only the Mohawk. Which has something extremely soft and musical in it when spoken by a woman. This Squaw is an expense of three or four thousand a year to the British Government as I am informed. She has a fine house building at Carleton Island, where several of her daughters live with her and a number of dependents. She was now in a traveling dress, a Calico Bedgown, fastened with Silver Brooches and a worsted mantel.[153]

That Brant could speak English is established a few years later in her travels with the wife of the lieutenant-governor of Upper Canada, Mrs. Elizabeth Simcoe. Here, however, she may have chosen not to do so since Butler spoke Mohawk. Even though Schieffelin's story contains errors, it provides a striking picture of Molly Brant at the age of forty-four. Once again, she was dressed in a combination of styles fabricated from European cloth. This included a bedgown, a loose jacket-like piece without fastenings which was worn by most eighteenth-century women. Indian women by this period had adopted the bedgown. Thus, Brant's fastening such a garment with silver trade broaches (worn only by Indians) combined items from two

---

(Lt. Col. Daniel Claus to Gen. Haldimand, Nov. 5, 1778, *Sir Frederick Haldimand: Unpublished Papers and Correspondence 1758-84,* Add. MSS 21774, Reel 51, pp. 11-14, World Microfilms Publications Ltd., London, England. © The British Library: 1977).

[152] Gilbert Tice to Claus, Feb. 12, 1780, *Claus Papers,* MG19, F1, 2:173, 175, transcribed by Wanda Burch.

[153] Matilda (Hanna) Lawrence Schieffelin to John Lawrence, Dec. 4, 1780, L. Effingham De Forest (ed.), "Hanna Lawrence Schieffelin's Letter," *The New York Genealogical and Biographical Record,* LXXII, No. 2 (1941), pp. 120–23.

Top: Remains of chimneys (Fort Haldimand) on Carleton Island, c. 1905; as illustrated on a post card published that year by the "Rotograph Co., NY."

Bottom: Aerial view, c. 1978, to the north showing the head of Carleton Island (Town of Cape Vincent, New York), with South and North Bay and Fort Haldimand.
Illustrations courtesy, New York State Office of Parks, Recreation and Historic Preservation; Bureau of Field Services.

cultures.[154] This may have been her habit her entire life except for formal occasions at Johnson Hall.

Hostilities between the Americans and the British formally ended with the peace treaty of 1783. The document contained no mention of the Six Nations and no attempt was made to protect their right to native lands, despite many British promises to do so. Brant's reaction must have been bitter. She had spent nearly eight years of her life traveling and cajoling the Iroquois to remain active in the British cause. Now, all of her inheritance and that of her children was lost. Other Indian leaders were not silent; they protested angrily, as did many of their fellow military and political allies.[155] In the end, they were granted land in Canada to replace that which they had lost, and they were given financial compensation.

---

[154] Information about clothing was provided by Robin Campbell, Curator at the New York State Office of Parks, Recreation and Historic Preservation, Bureau of Historic Sites, Peebles Island, Waterford, and, George Hamell, Senior Museum Exhibits Planner in Anthropology at the New York State Museum, Albany.

[155] Barbara Graymont, *The Iroquois in the American Revolution* (Syracuse, NY: 1972), pp. 259–62.

View of Cataraqui, by James Peachey. *Courtesy, National Archives of Canada, Ottawa.*

Saint George's Church (now St. Paul's), Kingston. Depicted in the insert is Rev. Dr. John Stuart. From a sketch produced by Gerry Lockin, Kingston, Ontario.

Chapter Six
KINGSTON

Molly Brant made one last move to the fort at Cataraqui and the newly established town of Kingston, in present day Ontario. There, in 1784, outside the walls of the fort, she settled into a house built for her by the British government. Nearby stood lodging built for her brother. Joseph Brant did not stay long in Kingston, though, preferring to live at the Grand River settlement established just north of Lake Erie. However, Joseph maintained his house at Kingston for use during frequent visits to his sister and his many friends there.[156] The new settlement by 1795 was described by a visitor as:

> ... considered a town ... Kingston may contain a few more buildings [than Newark, now Niagara-on-the-Lake, at the mouth of the Niagara River] but they are neither as large nor as good .... many of them are log–houses, and those which consist of joiner's work, are badly constructed and painted .... No town hall, no court–house, and no prison have hitherto been constructed .... The town is seated on rocky ground; and not the smallest house can be built without the foundation being excavated in a rock .... There is but one church in Kingston, and this, though very lately built, resembles a barn more than a church.[157]

This account describes Kingston as it was the year before Molly Brant's death. At the age of fifty-nine she was once again living in a frontier setting as she had when first moving to Johnson Hall. There, she and Johnson had to complete the Hall and build a town nearby with craftsmen's houses, a courthouse, a jail and a church. One wonders how she reacted to starting over again. Was it a familiar challenge, or was she tired of the struggle? Furnishing her new house in the manner she preferred must have been difficult, not just financially but in obtaining the goods she desired.[158]

---

[156] Kevin Quinn, "Joseph Brant: Kingston's Founding Father?," *Historic Kingston,* XXVIII (Kingston, ON: 1979), pp. 80–81.

[157] François Alexandre Frederic duc de la Rochefoucault-Liancourt, *Travels Through the United States of North America, the Country of the Iroquois, and Upper Canada in the Years 1795, 1796, and 1797* (London: 1799), pp. 279, 286, 287.

[158] The site of Brant's house was excavated by archaeologists in 1989. Although it had been destroyed by development, artifacts and features dating to her occupation were found. Cataraqui Archaeological Research Foundation, *Rideaucrest Development Property Mitigation Bb Gc-19* (Kingston, ON: 1989).

The Reverend Dr. John Stuart, considered the founding father of the Anglican Church in Upper Canada. Stuart, along with Molly Brant, was added to the Calendar of the Anglican Church of Canada in 1994. *Courtesy, National Archives of Canada, Ottawa.*

A pension of £100 a year was settled on her "in consideration of the early and uniform fidelity, attachment and zealous Services rendered to the King's Government by Miss Mary Brant and her Family."[159] Sir John Johnson, as Superintendent General and Inspector General of Indian Affairs, was to pay the pension quarterly. A few years later, Molly and her family also received compensation for their war losses. Guy Johnson, John Johnson, Daniel Claus, Joseph Chew and John Butler all testified on behalf of the children in order to establish their Loyalist claims. Molly Brant continued her contacts with the Johnson family. In June 1787, Sir John wrote to Joseph Brant that "your sister is here and Mrs. Kerr both with us and the children."[160] Mrs. Kerr was Molly's daughter Elizabeth who had married a doctor in 1783.

Molly Brant's son–in–law, John Ferguson, claimed in a petition filed in 1797 that, in the year 1785, she "went to Schenectady at which time great offers were made to Her, by the same people [the Americans] if She and Her Family would return to that Country, and about three years ago, they offered to Her and to such of Her Children as would return a sum of Money equal to the Sum their lands were sold for by the Commissioners of Confiscation.... That these offers, altho' so very great were rejected with the utmost contempt."[161] No confirmation has been found of such a trip, but Joseph Brant also declared in 1797 that he had been offered a pension for life by the Americans in 1785 if he would return.[162] During and immediately after the war, many Americans had moved onto former Indian land. Before 1786 the family knew that their lands were being sold and that "No Part Thereof will Ever be Restored to the Said Children."[163]

Very active in the Anglican community of Kingston, Molly Brant was the only woman listed in the 1792 founding charter of the church established there by the Reverend John Stuart, former minister at Fort Hunter.[164] In the same year a traveler, John C. Ogden, recorded seeing her there:

> ... *we saw an Indian woman, who sat in an honourable place among the English. She appeared very devout during*

[159] Haldimand to John Johnson, May 27, 1783, *Haldimand Papers,* Add. MSS 21775, p. 124.

[160] Haldimand to Joseph Brant, May 27, 1783 in Johnston, "Molly Brant," p. 104; National Archives of Canada, *Brant Family Papers,* Vol. I.

[161] The Memorial of John Ferguson, "Petitions for Grants of Land in Upper Canada, Second Series, 1796-99." With an introduction and notes by E. A. Cruikshank, *Ontario Historical Society Papers and Records,* XXVI (1930), p. 177. Quoted (imprecisely) also in Gundy, p. 106.

[162] Kelsay, pp. 369, 696 n66.

[163] Joseph Chew's Memorial to the Commissioners Appointed to Enquire into Losses and Services of American Loyalists, March 13 and 15, 1786. Transcribed from microfilm provided by Public Record Office, Audit Office 13, Vol. 11[2]-12[1], London.

[164] Anglican Diocese of Ontario, *The Cathedral Church of St. George* (Kingston, ON: 1989). This booklet is given to visitors to the church. There also is a plaque on the wall inside that lists the charter members.

**John Graves Simcoe,
Lieutenant-Governor
of Upper Canada.**

**Elizabeth Simcoe,
wife of
Lieutenant-Governor
John Graves Simcoe.
Molly Brant was a
frequent guest of
Gov. and Mrs. Simcoe.**

Both illustrations are from *The Diary of Mrs. John Graves Simcoe* **(J. Ross Robertson
[ed.], Toronto: 1934), based on miniatures at Wolford, Devon; artist unknown.**
*Courtesy, Special Collections, James A. Gibson Library, Brock University, St. Catharines,
Ontario.*

divine service, and very attentive to the sermon. She was the relict of the late Sir William Johnston, superintendant of Indian affairs, in the then province of New-York, and mother of several children by him who are married to Englishmen, and provided for by the crown. She is a sister to the celebrated Col. Brant, and has always been a faithful and useful friend in Indian affairs, while she resided in Johnston hall, and since her removal to Upper Canada. When Indian embassies arrived, she was sent for, dined at governor Simcoe's and treated with respect by himself, his lady, and family ... She retains the habit of her country women, and is a Protestant. During the life of Sir William, she was attended with splendor and respect, and since the war, receives a pension and compensation for losses, for herself and her children.[165]

She continued to be active in political as well as domestic spheres. In 1793, Brant was again at Fort Niagara, probably for two purposes. Her daughter Susanna was married there on June 5, and there was an important conference with American commissioners scheduled for the same week in Sandusky, Ohio. One of those attending a dance in honor of the King's birthday was American commissioner General Benjamin Lincoln who wrote:

In the evening there was quite a splendid ball, about twenty well dressed and handsome ladies, and about three times that number of gentlemen present.... What excited the best feelings of my heart was the ease and affection which which [sic] the ladies met each other, although there were a number present whose mothers sprang from the aborigines of the country. They appeared as well dressed as the company in general, and intermixed with them in a measure which evinced at once the dignity of their own minds, and the good sense of the others. These ladies possessed great ingenuity and industry, and have great merit; for the education they have acquired is owing principally to their own industry, as their father, Sir William Johnson, was dead and the mother retained the manners and dress of her tribe.[166]

It is not clear whether Brant was present at the ball, but she very likely was and was apparently dressed in Mohawk style. She and her daughters enjoyed an important position in their social and political world of the early 1790s.

---

[165] Ogden, p. 61.

[166] Journal of Gen. Benjamin Lincoln, June 4, 1793, *Hamilton Papers,* Box 2, Folder 12; Marjorie Freeman Campbell, *Niagara, Hinge of the Golden Arc* (Toronto: 1958), p. 166.

The Mohawk village on the Grand River (now Brantford, Ontario). This view was copied by Elizabeth Simcoe in 1793 from a sketch by Robert Pilkington. The large house on the left is probably Joseph Brant's, and the steeple of the still-extant Anglican church can be seen on the right. *Courtesy, The Archives of Ontario, Toronto (Simcoe Sketch No. 75).*

This 1807 engraving by George Heriot was entitled "Domesticated Indians of Canada" and depicts people who were probably Iroquois. *Courtesy, National Archives of Canada, Ottawa (C-12781).*

The following year, Molly Brant was once again at Niagara. Elizabeth Simcoe, wife of the lieutenant-governor of Upper Canada, John Graves Simcoe, was traveling from Niagara on a boat reserved for her personal use. However, as she related, "I relented in favour of Brant's sister who was ill and very desirous to go. She speaks English well & is a civil & very sensible old woman."[167] Here is Molly at age fifty-eight, still strong–willed and winning acceptance as a member of polite society, skills she turned to advantage whenever necessary. She frequently went to the Simcoe home for dinner and at one point was even called upon to use her medicinal skills to help the governor. In April 1795, Mrs. Simcoe recorded, "there was no medical advice but that of a Horse Doctor who pretended to be an apothecary." Molly accordingly "prescribed a Root - I believe it is calamus - which really relieved his Cough in a very short time."[168]

Brant suffered more losses during her last years in Kingston. Her loyal friend, Daniel Claus, died in 1787. Her daughters Elizabeth and Susanna both died in the early 1790s. By living in Kingston, Molly had isolated herself from many other Iroquois who had elected to live at Grand River with her brother Joseph, or at the Tyendinaga Reserve, near Deseronto, on the Bay of Quinté (about 30 miles west of Kingston). As a result, she lost some of her influence among them, but at this point in her life she preferred to emphasize her domestic role.

Molly Brant died in Kingston on April 16, 1796, at which time she was about sixty years old. She was buried in St. George's (now St. Paul's) church yard, but the exact location of her burial plot is today unknown. In 1986, to recognize her influential role in colonial history, Canada issued a commemorative stamp in her honor. The face pictured on the stamp is an idealization of the real person about whom so much myth evolved, even in her own lifetime.

---

[167] Mary Quayle Innis (ed.), *Mrs. Simcoe's Diary* (Toronto: 1965), p. 136.

[168] *Ibid.,* p. 155.

Mrs. William Johnson Kerr (Elizabeth Brant, daughter of Joseph Brant and his third wife, Catherine). William Johnson Kerr was the son of Molly's daughter Elizabeth and her husband, Dr. Robert Kerr. William and his wife were also first cousins . *Courtesy, Metropolitan Toronto Library Board (T31109).*

Chapter Seven
THE CHILDREN

In the 1830s, one of Molly Brant's daughters visited Johnson Hall for the first time since she had left it as a child. This probably was Margaret Farley who in 1831 was on her way to England to join her own children.[169] The visit was described by a Mr. Wells, who then lived at Johnson Hall, to Jeptha Simms, Mohawk Valley historian: "Mr. Wells said there had been an old woman about there looking at the building – said she got out in front of it and looking at the Hall said, 'O how I have lied about this house in Canada.' She had told people it was larger than any in Montreal.... she had gone from her residence at Johnson Hall at the age of about 10 years, and carried her juvenile recollections of it, as the largest house in all the land."[170] This charming tale provides a kind of closure to the story of Molly Brant and her children. Forced to leave the Mohawk Valley and the vast inheritances they were promised, the children all suffered through years of warfare, irregular schooling, uncertainty, and separation from each other before finding new homes in Upper Canada. In many ways, they too, are unsung heroes and victims of events not at all of their own making.

It is apparent that William Johnson and Molly Brant had great plans for their children. All were left vast estates, some already developed, so that they would have incomes. The undeveloped lands all connected with each other as though they were part of an overall development plan for the tract known as "Kingsland," something Sir William had not found time to do. The land holdings would make Peter and George great landlords; the girls would be heiresses. Powerful white males, all fellow Masons and members of Johnson's Indian Department, were appointed as their guardians: John Butler, Jelles Fonda, John Dease, James Stevenson, Henry Frey and Joseph Chew. Johnson expressed "full confidence" in these men, that "the Strong dependence on, & expectation of which unburthens my mind, allays my cares, & makes a change the less alarming."[171] These men were to administer a sum of money, the interest of which, along with the income

---

[169] Simms, however, reported the date as "I think it was in 1838," but that would have been too late for Margaret Farley to have been the visitor. Jean Johnston in "Ancestry and Descendants of Molly Brant," *Ontario History,* LXIII, No. 2 (June 1971), p. 91, is firm about the 1831 date but provides no source.

[170] *Draper Collection, Brant Manuscripts,* 13F175, p. 175, State Historical Society of Wisconsin, Madison. Microfilm copies in New York State Library, Albany.

[171] Will of Sir William Johnson, Jan. 27, 1774, *SWJP,* XII, p. 1075.

from their other legacies, was to be used for the children's education and maintenance until they came of age or married.

It is unclear whether the children all would have been allowed to pass on their inheritances to their heirs. Johnson's will called for this only in the case of Elizabeth's, George's and Anne's legacies — surely an oversight on his part. In August 1774, lawyer Peter Silvester wrote that, in his opinion, the other children, even Peter, would have their estates only for life. Sir John Johnson provided lawyer James Duane with a copy of the will in an effort to break the entail in 1775.[172] Sir William's will specified that "no part" of the land in Kingsland "be ever sold by those to whom I have divised it." Apparently Sir John was trying to break that clause so that all of the children could have a freer hand in the future. Silvester's legal opinion might have related to the entail problem. In the end, all of their Loyalist awards were based on the value of the holdings specified in Johnson's will. Apparently, some legal recognition was given to the legatees of Johnson's will as late as the 1790s. In 1795, Moses Johnson, eldest son and heir of William of Canajoharie, Sir William's son, signed an indenture granting to Douw Fonda one thousand acres of land in the Kingsland grant which he had inherited from his father who had inherited it from Sir William Johnson. Moses was listed as living in Upper Canada, Douw Fonda as living in Johnstown.[173]

• Peter •

The eldest, Peter Warren Johnson, born in September 1759, made the ultimate sacrifice: he died during the early years of the Revolutionary War while fighting for the British. As detailed earlier, Peter was being prepared by his parents for a life in merchandising. In addition, however, he was to have four large land grants in the Mohawk Valley that already included buildings, mills and other improvements. Upon his mother's death, he was to inherit her holdings. Thus, Peter was to be a great landlord. As part of his training and refinement as an eighteenth-century gentleman, he had been sent to several schools where he was taught to read and write in English, Mohawk and French, and to play the violin.

Before his death Peter was also recognized as a military leader. As a result of his exploits near Montreal, Governor Tryon had even suggested he be made a general. Peter was then seventeen. His death in 1777 was a tragic loss to his mother and to history. His parents obviously intended that he should be a leader in the Mohawk Valley society they were helping to create. He was expected to participate both in the white and Mohawk worlds. It is fascinating to speculate what might have happened. Following his death, the captive, William Lamb, Jr. may have been adopted by Molly Brant as a "substitute" for Peter.

---

[172] Will of Sir William Johnson, Jan. 27, 1774, SWJP, XII, p. 1062, n1. An entail is an inheritance assigned to a specific line of heirs in such a way that it can never be legally transferred.

[173] Indenture made May 29, 1795, Hamilton Papers, Box 1, Folder 28.

• *Elizabeth* •

Elizabeth Johnson was the oldest girl, born about 1763.[174] She was close to her mother and may have functioned as her amanuensis, at least when corresponding in English. She was learning to sew while living at Johnson Hall and apparently, along with her sisters, became very proficient. Captain Joseph Bloomfield himself purchased some of their handiwork while visiting the family at Canajoharie in 1776, and she probably was the daughter he described as being "Very handsome" and "richly dressed agreable to the Indian–Fashion."[175] Elizabeth probably attended school in Johnstown, and did attend school in Schenectady while living at Canajoharie. She also was to inherit land: 700 acres on the north side of the Mohawk which already had buildings and other improvements and 2,000 acres next to one of the grants given to her brother Peter. Interestingly, Johnson specified that Elizabeth could pass on her legacy only to "heirs lawfully begotten," an interesting phrase for Sir William to use!

Once marriageable, Elizabeth was popular at balls held both at Carleton Island and at Niagara after the war. She married Dr. Robert Kerr at Niagara in 1783, sometime after November 26, when she was still listed as Elizabeth Johnson living at Carleton Island with her mother. Robert Kerr, a native of Scotland who had served under Burgoyne in 1777, was a physician and magistrate.[176] Elizabeth and Robert had five children, some of whom traveled with their mother and Molly to visit Sir John Johnson in 1787. Elizabeth died in 1794, at only thirty-two years of age, while giving birth to her son, Robert J. Kerr.[177] This was another tragic loss for Molly Brant, whose own death followed two years later. Elizabeth's husband never remarried. In the late 1790s Joseph Brant tried to obtain an official appointment for Kerr to live among the Mohawk as their physician.[178] Kerr practiced medicine in the Indian Department and in other military departments until at least 1820 and maintained his private practice as well. His house and barn at Niagara, Upper Canada (present day Niagara-on-the-Lake), were burned during the War of 1812 while he was serving as a doctor for the British forces. In 1823, he moved to Albany, New York, where he died the next year at the age of sixty-nine.[179] One of their sons, William Johnson Kerr, married his first cousin, Elizabeth Brant, daughter of Joseph and his

---

[174] The birth dates of all of the children born after Peter are given variously by secondary sources. The most important primary document is the "Return of Loyalists on Carleton Island," Nov. 1783, *Haldimand Papers,* Add. MSS 21787, p. 344.

[175] Journal of Joseph Bloomfield, July 14, 1776, Lender and Martin, p. 72.

[176] Johnston, "Ancestry and Descendants of Molly Brant," p. 90.

[177] Draper Collection, 13F99.

[178] Kelsay, p. 530. For additional information on Kerr's medical career, see William Colgate, "Dr. Robert Kerr: An Early Practitoner of Upper Canada," *The Canadian Medical Association Journal,* No. 64 (1951), pp.542-46. The article also gives information on a variety of other timely events.

third wife Catherine. The youngest son, Robert J. Kerr, married his first cousin, Mary Farley, daughter of Margaret Johnson Farley and Captain George Farley. Obviously, these families remained close. In 1830, Robert J. Kerr, a physician like his father, had the artist John George Kingston make a copy of a portrait of Peter Warren Johnson. The copy now hangs in the John Ross Robertson Collection in the Toronto Public Library.[180] Perhaps it was done in memory of Elizabeth who was so close to her brother Peter.

• *Magdalene* •

Magdalene Johnson, born in 1765, was two years younger than Elizabeth. She too was educated in Johnstown and Schenectady and, along with her sister and mother, was admired as a seamstress by Captain Bloomfield. Magdalene was to inherit developed land consisting of 900 acres and 2,000 more that was undeveloped but adjoining that of her sister Elizabeth. Magdalene was eighteen while living at Carleton Island in 1783 and was one of the two daughters considered marriageable except for the lack of a dowry. She did marry John Ferguson who became a member of the Legislature of Upper Canada for Kingston. She and Ferguson had no surviving children, and Magdalene died in 1818.[181] Molly Brant was living with the Fergusons in Kingston when she herself died in 1796.

• *Margaret* •

Margaret Johnson, born in 1767, was the early nineteenth-century visitor to Johnson Hall and also the author of "Testimony of a Child of Molly Brant"[182] in which she described the family's experiences at Canajoharie. Margaret, probably named for Molly Brant's mother, was to inherit 230 acres in the Stone Arabia patent and 2,000 acres in the Kingsland patent next to that of Magdalene. Margaret married Captain George Farley of the 24th Regiment of Foot, and they had four children. One of these, Mary Ann, married her cousin Robert Kerr. The Kerrs and two of Margaret's other children went to England to live where she joined them in 1831. Margaret died there in 1844.

• *George* •

George Johnson was the second son, born in 1768. He was six years old when he left Johnson Hall and about nine years old when they fled from Canajoharie. William Lamb, the captive living with Molly Brant and her children at Carleton Island, may have been servant to George since they

---

[179] *Dictionary of Canadian Biography, VI,* pp. 374–75.

[180] "The Johnson Portraits," *SWJP,* XIII, p. xii.

[181] Johnston, "Ancestry and Descendants of Molly Brant," p. 90.

[182] "Testimony of a Child of Molly Brant," March 15, 1841, transcribed by Milton Hamilton, Albany Institute of History & Art, *Hamilton Papers,* Box 2, Folder 12.

were close in age. George Johnson went to school in Montreal where his instructors and his uncle Daniel Claus expressed great satisfaction with his abilities. George would have inherited from his father 530 acres of improved land in the Sacandaga patent and 2,000 acres next to that of his sister Margaret in the Kingsland patent. The amount of improved land was about twice that given to his individual sisters and about half that to be received by Peter. George also was to pass on his land to heirs "lawfully begotten."

Little is known of George Johnson's life after the war except for an affidavit filed in 1818 in which he tried to establish a claim to his deceased sister Magdelene Ferguson's property. Family recollections recorded by Lyman C. Draper state that he died in 1826 and was buried three miles above Brantford. He was a "nice man" and was once a Methodist exhorter. Others said he lived an Indian life and was thought to be indolent and shiftless. Another said he married a Mohawk and lived at Grand River. This same informant called him "Big George." Still another claimed he was a well educated person who taught school for many years between Brantford and Paris, Ontario. Although not a sachem, chief or man of prominence, he had an excellent character. Finally, one informant remembered that George died in 1822 on the banks of Grand River two miles west of Brantford. He taught day school, not the Mohawk School. His widow then remarried but died about 1855, again with no issue. This informant also called him "Big George" and said he was sixty years old when he died.[183] The charter of the Anglican church founded in Kingston in 1792 lists George Johnson as one of its founders. He was then twenty-four years of age.

• *Mary* •

Mary Johnson was born at Johnson Hall in 1771. She would have remembered little of her life there, as she departed at the age of three. Mary was to inherit 150 acres of developed land in the Stone Arabia patent and 2,000 next to those of her brother George in the Kingsland patent. She was educated in Montreal and never married. Mary died in 1813 at the age of forty–four. After her sister Susanna's death in 1795, Mary's hand in marriage was requested by her widowed brother-in-law, Henry LeMoine. When this arrangement was refused, LeMoine shot himself to death on June 24, 1796, supposedly in the parlor of the Ferguson home.[184] Mary was described by a family member as "a very handsome spinster & a perfect Lady."[185]

---

[183] All of these family stories are from the *Draper Collection,* 13F 29, 94, 130; 14F24, 27, 67–68.

[184] William D. Reid, *The Loyalists in Ontario: The Sons and Daughters of the American Loyalists of Upper Canada* (Lambertville, NJ: 1973), p. 33; *Draper Collection,* F1392, 130, 147, 92. Family informants claim that Molly Brant helped make the decision not to grant LeMoine's wish. Mrs. Ferguson was so strongly opposed because of LeMoine's ill treatment of his first wife. However, the suicide took place after Molly's death, so she was spared this tragedy.

[185] *Draper Collection,* 13F188.

Plaque on the exterior wall of St. Paul's Church, Kingston, Ontario, facing the cemetery.

Part of the cemetery at St. Paul's Church, Kingston, Ontario, which includes the burial place of Molly Brant. The exact spot of her grave is unknown.

• *Susanna* •

Susanna Johnson was perhaps named for Uncle Peter Warren's wife. Born in 1772, Susanna was to inherit 3,000 acres of unimproved land in the Kingsland patent next to Mary's tract. She was educated in Montreal and married Ensign Henry LeMoine of the 60th (Royal American) Regiment of Foot on June 5, 1793 while her mother was visiting at Niagara.[186] Upon Susanna's death, LeMoine attempted to marry her sister Mary.

• *Anne* •

Named perhaps for Daniel Claus' wife and Sir William's mother, Anne was born in 1773. She was a year old when she left Johnson Hall and was only four when the family fled from Canajoharie. Anne also was to inherit only unimproved land: 3,000 acres in the Kingsland patent next to that of her sister Susanna, land which could be passed on to heirs lawfully begotten. Anne married "a naval officer, Captain Hugh Earl for whom Earl Street in Kingston, Ontario is named."[187] They had three daughters. Anne died in 1818. None of her daughters produced children.

Résumé

It is clear from the above biographies that Molly's and Sir William's children had overcome tremendous odds during their lifetimes. Snatched from the Valley that was to have provided them with a homeland, both by virtue of their Mohawk inheritance and their father's generosity, they had to accept the momentous changes brought by war and revolution. Molly Brant's strong will not only helped each child with this task, but they learned from her to have strengths of their own. Although the girls all married non-Indians, they obviously kept their family attachments to Joseph Brant, John Johnson and other individuals involved in the Indian Department in Canada. For example, by June 1818 Daniel Claus' son, William, was Deputy Superintendent of Indian Affairs. On that date, he certified that William J. Kerr had been captain of the Western Indians and Six Nations Indians during a military engagement fought in June 1813. "None were engaged with the enemy [American forces] that day but the ... Indians and about 180 of the Seven Nations from the Province of Lower Canada."[188] Once again the Iroquois were assisting the British, and once again many of the same family members were involved. William Claus was Sir William Johnson's grandson and namesake. William Johnson Kerr was Sir William's and Molly Brant's grandson who would marry Joseph Brant's daughter in 1824. Thus, the families not only intermarried but also remained aware of their Mohawk heritage.

---

[186] Johnston, "Ancestry and Descendants of Molly Brant," p. 90.; Reid, p. 33.

[187] Johnston, "Ancestry and Descendants of Molly Brant," p. 90.

[188] William Claus's Certification of William J. Kerr, June 24, 1818, *Brant Family Papers* 1:83. This reference is to the Battle of Beaverdams, fought on June 24, 1813, near present day Thorold, Ontario.

Johnson Hall, rear view. *Courtesy, New York State Office of Parks, Recreation and Historic Preservation; Johnson Hall State Historic Site.*

Sir William Johnson's Courthouse at Johnstown. *Courtesy, New York State Office of Parks, Recreation and Historic Preservation; Johnson Hall State Historic Site.*

Chapter Eight
CONCLUSIONS

Molly Brant was described by her contemporaries as handsome, sensible, judicious, political, faithful, prudent, likely, well bred, pleasant, delightful, an uncommonly agreeable person, having good understanding, having great art, being at ease in society, capable of scolding, influential, of great use, pretty large minded, zealous, having a violent temper, being capable of mischief (trouble), civil, devout and respected. This great variety of descriptions by eighteenth century contemporaries demonstrates that she was a woman of many dimensions. As a woman, mother, and political force, she was a legend in her own century. For fifteen years, she was a vital link between the Iroquois and Sir William Johnson in the management of Indian affairs. Then, for the next ten, she acted as intermediary and conduit between her people and the British government. At the same time, she had to provide for eight children, see to their education and try to regain some of the fortune they had lost. Her choice of political roles during this time is controversial; her success in her domestic role is admirable. Today she is seen by the Canadians as a founder. In the United States, however, her Loyalist activities have tended to overshadow her fascinating personal story. Unlike Pocahontas and Sacajawea, Indian heroines familiar to the American public, Molly Brant has never been a highly visible figure.

Visitors to Johnson Hall State Historic Site in Johnstown, New York, in the 1960s were told that Brant was an evil concubine whose charms Johnson found irresistible. In the 1930s, she was seen as "a forest child" who experienced an "astonishing evolution" from "wigwam housekeeping" to life at the Hall.[189] Today Johnson Hall is interpreted as the home of both Sir William Johnson and Molly Brant. In addition to Johnson's life and accomplishments, Brant's roles as housekeeper, hostess and mother, together with her influence in the management of colonial Indian affairs, are emphasized. From primary sources, such as the 1774 inventory and visitors' descriptions, the house is being furnished to reflect both their cultures. While giving tours, staff members discuss domestic life at Johnson Hall and Molly Brant's role in making the Hall the unique place it was. Here a baronet and a Native American woman lived together as partners, raised a family, and exercised great political power.

Fort Johnson, too, is open to the public. There, emphasis is placed on Johnson's earlier life and military exploits. Canajoharie today is a grassy

---

[189] Pound, p. 141.

**Engraving (woodcut) of the Indian Castle Church (at Canajoharie) depicting its
original 18th Century appearance. Alterations were made during an 1855 restoration. From Benson J. Lossing's** *Pictorial Field-Book of the Revolution.*

knoll readily identifiable from the New York State Thruway by the still-standing Indian Castle Church, built originally in 1769 by Sir William Johnson. The structure there today was remodeled in 1855. Archaeological excavations at the Indian Castle Church in 1972 revealed that the structure had been turned about eighty-five degrees in the nineteenth century to align it with the road. The church built by Johnson had been aligned with the compass (the long walls facing north and south, and the short walls facing east and west).[190] One of the short walls of the church now faces north. The entrance into Johnson's church was on a long side; it is now on the short north facade. The roof still retains its steep eighteenth-century pitch. It is a charming building and is open to the public. Also still standing at Canajoharie is the Dutch barn once used by the Brant family. Visible from the Thruway, it was restored in 1994.

Fort Niagara is open to the public. Although renovated for military purposes many times, extensive documentary and archaeological work there has established the location of many earlier buildings. Fort Niagara emphasizes all the time periods of its occupation and thus has living history programs reflecting these interpretations. Carleton Island today is a privately owned undeveloped area, accessible only by boat. The remains of the fort are still visible even from the water.

Kingston, Ontario, is a thriving city, proud of its history. Museums, publications, walking tours, and almost continuous archaeological projects there have helped to keep that awareness alive. Molly Brant's Anglican church, now called St. Paul's, still stands, and her memory is kept alive there through interpretive signs, plaques and brochures. In 1994 the Anglican Church of Canada honored Molly Brant and the Reverend John Stuart by adding them to the church Calendar. With her name assigned to April 16, Molly Brant is commemorated on that day with special prayers. The Calendar also gives her national recognition. Referring to her as a "wise and prudent mother in the household of the Mohawk nation," the prayers mention her "gifts of justice and loyalty," her attributes as a "leader among her own people," and the strength she used "to gather and guide an exiled people."[191] Molly would have been pleased.

Molly Brant would not recognize most of these places today were she able to revisit them. However, she left her mark on each, and each was a part of her complex and fascinating story.

---

[190] Wayne Lenig, "Archaeology, Education and the Indian Castle Church," *The Bulletin of the New York State Archaeological Association,* LXIX (March 1977), pp. 47–49; Indian Castle Church Restoration and Preservation Society brochure.

[191] Stephen Reynolds, *For All the Saints; Prayers and Readings for Saints' Days According to the Calendar of the Book of Alternative Services of the Anglican Church of Canada* (Toronto: 1994), p. 145.

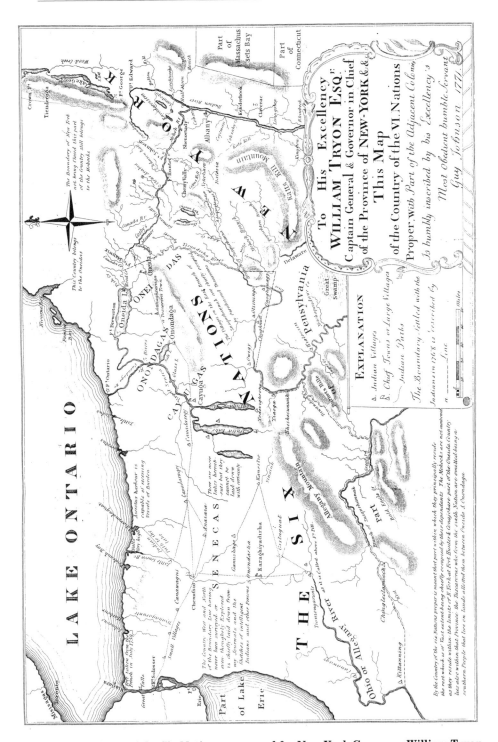

Map of the territory of the Six Nations, prepared for New York Governor William Tryon, by Guy Johnson (1771). From O'Callaghan's *Documentary History of New York.*

Appendix 'A'
CHRONOLOGY OF EVENTS
IN MOLLY BRANT'S LIFE

1735, Apr. 13	Mary, daughter of Margaret and Cannassware, baptised at Fort Hunter Church. (Kelsay, p. 40)
1736	Molly born? Date based on 1783 Return. (*Haldimand Papers,* Add MSS 21787, p. 344)
1738	William Johnson arrives from Ireland. (Hereafter referred to as...SWJ)
1743	Joseph Brant born. (Kelsay, p. 361)
1753	Molly's mother and Brant Canagaraduncka marry. (Kelsay, p. 57)
1754	Claus and Hendrick visit Esopus and Albany where Capt. Stairs falls in love with Molly Brant. (*Claus Papers,* Reel C, 23:36–37)
1759, Aug. 21	SWJ writes to Molly Brant not to come to Oswego. (*SWJP,* XIII, p. 125)
1759, Sept. 10	SWJ sends letter to Molly and one to daughter Nancy. (*SWJP,* XIII, p. 139)
1759, Sept.	Peter Warren Johnson born. (Hamilton 1975)
1761, Oct.	Daughter born to Molly Brant and SWJ. (*SWJP,* XIII, p. 271)
1763	Elizabeth born. Date based on 1783 Return. (*Haldimand Papers,* Add MSS 21787, p. 344)
1765	Magdalene born. Date based on 1783 Return. (*Haldimand Papers,* Add MSS 21787, p. 344)
1764, Feb. 19	W. Marsh gives compliments to Chgiagh [Molly]. (*SWJP,* XI, p. 72)

1764, Apr. 2	Cash for "Mrs. Moley" in J. Butler's Account Book. (*SWJP*, XIII, p. 508)
1764, Aug. 4	Trinkets sent from London for Molly and the children by Croghan. (*SWJP*, IV, p. 501)
1765	Lord Adam Gordon sends love to Molly and thanks for breakfast. (*SWJP*, XIII, p. 376)
1765, June	Lady Susan O'Brien entertained; describes Molly Brant as "well–bred and pleasant lady." (Stone , II, p. 244)
1766	Cash for Mrs. Mary and 12 pounds butter for Jacobes Kneff per her order in John Butler's Account Book. (*SWJP*, XIII, p. 515)
1767	Margaret born. Date based on 1783 Return. (*Haldimand Papers,* Add MSS 21787, p. 344)
1769	George born. Date based on 1783 Return. (*Haldimand Papers,* Add MSS 21787, p. 344)
1768, Nov. 17	Apology from Wetherhead for taking leave without saying good–bye to Molly. (*SWJP*, VI, p. 463)
1769, Jan. 23	Two blankets for Molly sent by MacLeod from Niagara. (*SWJP*, VI, p. 604)
1769	J. Fonda's Account: 1 lock for Molly from Dec. 10, 1769. (*SWJP*, VII, p. 973)
1769	Church at Canajoharie built by SWJ. (*SWJP*, XII, p. 894; Kelsay, p. 132)
1769, Sept. 17	Two children baptized at Johnson Hall. (Records of St. Peter's Church: 101, Albany)
1769, Dec. 31	Two children baptized at Johnson Hall. (Records of St. Peter's Church: 102, Albany)
1770, Jan. 28	One child baptized at Johnson Hall. (Records of St. Peter's Church: 102, Albany)
1770, Feb. 9	Oquaga Indian's wife and her sister salute Molly. (*SWJP*, VII, p. 379)

1770, Feb. 21	John van Epps sends a leg of venison for Molly. (*SWJP,* VII, p. 409)
1770, March 4	Two children baptized at SWJ's church, one white, one Indian. Two more at SWJ's house, both Indians, one of them daughter of Molly. (Records of St. Peter's Church: 102, Albany)
1770, May 18	Stevenson requests help with his son left with the Seneca. (*SWJP,* VIII, p. 974)
1770, June 20	Three children baptized at Johnson Hall. (Records of St. Peter's Church: 103, Albany)
1770, Aug. 25	As per order of Miss Molly: Wm. Fox sends bill for punch, rum, meals, pasture given to the Indians; also 24 pounds butter delivered to Margaret Brant as per SWJ's request. (*SWJP,* VII, p. 865)
1770, Sept. 28	Betsy Johnson buying sewing items. (*SWJP,* XIII, p. 563)
1771	Mary born. Date based on 1783 Return. (*Haldimand Papers,* Add MSS 21787, p. 344)
1771, Mar. 13	Stevenson requests Molly's help in getting a boy from the Seneca at some expense; asks her advice and assistance; writing from Detroit. (*SWJP,* VIII, p. 16)
1772	Susanna born. Date based on 1783 Return. (*Haldimand Papers,* Add MSS 21787, p. 344)
1772, Mar. 20	John Cottgrave, schoolteacher in Johnstown, discusses Peter Johnson's upcoming trip to Canada and his behavior in school. (*SWJP,* VIII, p. 424)
1772, Apr. 28, Sept. 15	Molly purchases cloth, ribbons, lace, etc. (*SWJP,* XIII, pp. 590, 597)
1772, March 8	Stevenson asks again about the child. (*SWJP,* VIII, p. 469)
1773	Anne born. Date based on 1783 Return. (*Haldimand Papers,* Add MSS 21787, p. 344)

1773, Apr. 12	Molly buys one dozen cups and saucers. (*SWJP,* XIII, p. 608)
1773, Nov. 18	Peter writes from Philadelphia where he is to be trained in business. (*SWJP,* XII, p. 1043)
1773, Dec. 13	Peter writes from Philadelphia. (*SWJP,* VIII, p. 945)
1773, Dec. 25	Stevenson thanks SWJ and Molly for pains taken about young warrior. (*SWJP,* VIII, p. 974)
1774, Jan. 27	SWJ makes his will leaving money, goods, and land to Molly Brant and the children. (*SWJP,* XII, pp. 1062ff)
1774, March 31	Stevenson sends compliments to Molly and thanks for pains she took relative to the child. (*SWJP,* VIII, p. 1103)
1774, Apr. 1	Stevenson asks Molly to flatter an Indian who is a rising star; mentions he would like to compose a small history of the Dutch connection with the Indians, naming the particular families who have the honor of having "savage blood" in their veins. (*SWJP,* VIII, p. 1108)
1774, Apr. 21	Letter from Peter Johnson at Philadelphia. (*SWJP,* XIII, p. 636)
1774, Apr. 30	Letter from Peter at Philadelphia. (*SWJP,* VIII, p. 1139)
1774	Daily activities at Johnson Hall described later by Judge Jones. (DeLancey, pp. 373–74)
1774?	Description of Molly and her roles written later by Jones. (DeLancey, p. 374)
1774, July 25	Probate date for will of SWJ. (*SWJP,* XII, p. 1062)
1774, Aug. 1	Opinions of lawyer P. Silvester written re SWJ's will as applied to Molly Brant and her children. (*SWJP,* VIII, pp. 1189, 1190, 1191)

1774, Aug. 2	"The things in Molly Brants Room" exempted from inventory. (*SWJP,* XIII, p. 647)
1775, Aug. 13	Molly at Canajoharie. (Harrison, p. 83)
1775, Aug. 15	Molly at German Flatts for conference. (Harrison, p. 86)
1775, Sept.	Peter in Montreal when Ethan Allen raided; helps take Allen prisoner. (*DRCHSNY,* VIII, p. 637)
1776, June 9	American troops march past Canajoharie and describe Molly Brant. (Lender and Martin, p. 61)
1776, June 17	Bloomfield calls on Molly Brant in Canajoharie. (Lender and Martin, p. 63)
1776, June 27	Elmer stops at Canajoharie to see the Misses Johnson. (Elmer, p. 132)
1776, July 14	Bloomfield buys leggings from Miss Molly and her daughters. (Lender and Martin, p. 72)
1776, July 18	Bloomfield says Indian women at German Flatts conference "are generally at work makeing Mockinsons & such other Things as they use themselves or expect to sell to us." (Lender and Martin, p. 77)
1776, Aug. 4	Bloomfield visited by "sundry Indian Ladies" for tea. (Lender and Martin, p. 96)
1777, Jan. 14	Kirkland writes that the Oneida told him Molly has written to her brother Joseph not to execute the current plan until she has time to escape in the spring. (Penrose, p. 67)
1777	Molly's child remembers their having to leave Canajoharie. (*Hamilton Papers*)
1777	Peter Johnson dies. (Kelsay, p. 272; *SWJP,* XII, p. 966n, *SWJP,* XIII, p. 1025n)

1777, Oct. 16	Claus reports that Molly Brant sent reports to Joseph Brant of rebel troops advancing which proved valuable at the Battle of Oriskany. (*DRCHSNY,* VIII, p. 721)
1777, Nov. 6	Claus reports Oneida took revenge on Molly Brant at Canajoharie forcing her and her family to flee to Onondaga. (*DRCHSNY,* VIII, p. 725)
1777	Claus writes that Butler sent messages to Molly Brant urging her to come and live at Niagara. (*Haldimand Papers,* Add MSS 21774, pp. 57–58)
1777	List of material goods left behind by the Brant family when they fled Canajoharie. (Guldenzopf, pp. 204–05)
1778	Claus writes to Sir John Johnson that Joseph and Molly Brant outdo fifty Butlers when it comes to managing Indians. (Johnston 1964, p. 116)
1778, Jan. 23	Joseph Brant writes to Claus from Niagara and sends compliments from Molly and her family. (Penrose, p. 106)
1778, Apr. 21	Affidavits about the plundering at Canajoharie lists goods taken from Molly Brant. (Penrose, p. 134)
1778, summer	Molly living in house ordered for her by Haldimand. (Johnston 1964, p. 117)
1778, June 23	Molly writes to Claus from Niagara to thank him for necessary articles he sent; sends love to the Clauses and Sir John and his Lady. (*Claus Papers,* MG19, F1, 2:29)
1778, Sept. 15	Claus mentions letter from Molly Brant dated Aug. 30 at Niagara. (Penrose, p. 155)
1778	Joseph Brant gives Molly £30, Haldimand £25. (Gundy, p. 101)

1778, Oct. 26	Merchants Taylor & Duffin describe Molly Brant at Niagara. (Penrose, p. 167)
1778, Nov. 5	Claus asks Molly Brant to deliver messages to Six Nations. (Penrose, p. 169)
1778, winter	Molly at Niagara; also mother Margaret; had been to Montreal; is unhappy with Col. Stacia [Stacey]. (W. Campbell, p. 182; Kelsay, p. 272)
1778, Dec. 23	Desorontyon tells Claus Molly wrote a letter to him in Mohawk. (*DHNY,* IV, p. 330)
1779, June	Col. Bolton at Niagara suggests Molly and her family be transferred to Montreal. (*Haldimand Papers,* Add MSS 21764, p. 18)
1779, July 16	Bolton writes that Molly and family will leave Niagara the next day. (Gundy, p. 102)
1779, Aug. 29	Claus visited by Molly in Montreal; she recounts her adventures. (*Haldimand Papers,* Add. MSS 21774, pp. 57–59)
1779, Sept. 6	Molly hears of Clinton and Sullivan campaign; wishes to go to Niagara. (*Haldimand Papers,* Add MSS 21174, p. 63)
1779, Sept. 9	Haldimand agrees Molly Brant can go to Niagara. (*Ibid.,* p. 65)
1779, Sept. 13	Molly on her way to Niagara; left 2 youngest girls with Claus for schooling. (*Ibid.,* pp. 67–68)
1779, Sept. 13	Haldimand writes to Secretary of State Lord Germain of Molly Brant's influence with the Six Nations. (*Haldimand Papers,* Add MSS 21714, p. 42)
1779	Clinton and Sullivan campaign ongoing; threatens Niagara. (Gundy, p. 102, n. 27)
1779, Oct. 5	Molly writes to Claus; she is at Carleton Island. (Claus Papers, MG19, F1, 2:135–36)

1779, Nov.	Sir John Johnson's expedition fails leaving hundreds of Indians to winter on Carleton Island; he is there himself Sept. 26. (Gundy, n. 37)
1779, Nov. 21	Guy Johnson complains about Molly Brant taking goods from the Stores; wishes to gratify her desires, but she is "pretty large minded." (*Hamilton Papers*)
1780, Feb. 12	Tice writes to Claus of life on Carleton Island and Molly Brant's help. (*Claus Papers,* MG19, F1, 2:173, 175)
1780. Feb. 23	Fraser writes from Carleton Island and encloses a letter from Molly Brant who has been very helpful. (*Claus Papers,* MG19, F1, 2:177)
1780, March 21	Fraser at Carleton Island praises Molly Brant's help with the Indians left there after the Clinton and Sullivan campaign. (*Haldimand Papers,* Add MSS 21787, p. 116)
1780, June 21	Fraser writes of Molly's unhappiness with living arrangements. (*Ibid.,* p. 150)
1780, June 26	Claus to John Johnson: Molly, George and others visiting him; plan to go to Quebec to see Haldimand personally; Claus suggests yearly payments of £200. (*Hamilton Papers*)
1780, June 29	John Johnson from Quebec: glad Molly safe; will do what he can to promote her interests; Molly should not come to Quebec. (*Claus Papers,* MG19, F1, 2:235)
1780, July 17	Haldimand from Quebec orders house to be built for Molly Brant within a few hundred yards of the fort on Carleton Island. (*Haldimand Papers,* Add MSS 21788, p. 94)
1780, Dec. 4	Matilda Schieffelin writes to her father about meeting Molly Brant near Fort Niagara. (De Forest, pp. 120–23)

1781	Fraser relieved by Major Ross. Writes of his special instructions for the care of Molly Brant who seems happy in her new house. (*Haldimand Papers,* Add MSS 21787, p. 201)
1781, Apr. 12	Molly writes to Claus from Carleton Island: worried about her brother. (*Haldimand Papers,* Add MSS 21774, p. 180)
1781, July 26	Molly brings back 3 children from school in Montreal. (*Haldimand Papers,* Add MSS 21774, p. 208)
1782, July 25	Molly again brings children home from school in Montreal. (*Ibid.,* p. 279)
1782, Oct. 11	Receipt signed "Wari" by Molly Brant. (*Haldimand Papers,* microfilm A684, p. 117)
1782, Nov.	Peace treaty signed; no stipulation on behalf of Six Nations. (Johnston 1964, p. 121)
1783, May	Joseph in London; pension of £100 authorized for Molly. (*Haldimand Papers,* Add MSS 21775, p. 124; Kelsay, p. 342)
1783, summer	Ross arrives at Cataraqui where he receives letter from Molly; asks Haldimand for house to be built for her. Approval given. (Gundy, p. 105, n. 49)
1783, summer	Joseph at Cataraqui; unhappy that house not ready. (Gundy, p. 105, n. 51)
1783, Nov. 26	List of rations drawn from the King's Store at Carleton Island. Lists Molly, 6 daughters, 3 slaves. Molly's age is 47 years. (*Haldimand Papers,* Add MSS 21787, p. 344)
1783/84	Elizabeth marries Dr. Robert Kerr.
1784, Feb. 17	Joseph happy with house being built for Molly. (Gundy, p. 106, n. 53) Brant's house is 40 feet by 30 feet, storey and a half. Molly's house almost complete. (Gundy, p. 106, n. 54)

1784–1790	Commission begins inquiry into Loyalists' claims. John Johnson appointed to supervise settlement of soldiers, refugees, Iroquois. (Johnston 1973, p. 107)
1785	Rev. Stuart arrives in Cataraqui with family. Services held in barracks. (Diocese of Ontario)
1786	Molly granted, with Joseph, sum of £1449, 14 shillings, 6 pence compensation for war losses. (Thomas, p. 147)
1786–88	Joseph Brant, Guy Johnson, John Butler and others testify to Molly's wartime contributions. (Fraser)
1787, June	Molly, Elizabeth Kerr, her children visit John Johnson. (Johnston 1973, p. 104)
1787, Aug	Molly witness for George House who served in Butlers' Rangers. (Fraser, p. 983)
1787	Molly's claim was for £1206. All the Mohawk got £15,000; Joseph got his and Molly's while in London. (Kelsay, p. 390)
1788, March	John Johnson appears as witness for the claims of his half–brother and half–sisters for the value of the land left them in SWJ's will. (Johnston 1964, p. 122)
1791	Magdalene in Kingston marries John Ferguson. (Reid, p. 33)
1792	Molly and son George listed as founders of church in Kingston. (Diocese of Ontario)
1792	Ogden observes Molly in church. (Ogden, p. 61)
1790s	Molly, son George and 2 sons–in–law among founders of new church in Kingston. (Thomas, p. 147)
1793, June 4	King's birthday ball; General Lincoln leaves description of Molly's daughters attending. (*Hamilton Papers;* Innis, p. 9)

1793, June 5	Susanna marries Ensign Henry LeMoine of the 60th Regiment of Foot. (Reid, p. 33)
1793, after March 30	Anne marries Capt. Hugh Earl. (C. File, no page numbers used)
1794, Jan. 24	Elizabeth dies at Niagara, age 32. (Reid, p. 33)
1794, Sept. 13	Mrs. Simcoe gives Molly a ride from Niagara to Kingston. (Innis, p. 136)
1795, Apr. 24	Molly treats Gov. Simcoe for cough. (Innis, p. 155)
1795, Dec. 28	Susanna dies at Kingston. (Reid, p. 33)
1796, April 16	Molly Brant dies in Kingston at Magdalene Ferguson's home. (Reid, p. 33)
1796, May 22	Joseph Chew writes that "My old friend Mrs. Brant died." (Burton, p. 449)
1797	Son–in–law Ferguson and Joseph Brant relate that Molly and Joseph were offered land grants and money to return to the Mohawk Valley. (Johnston 1973, p. 108; Gundy, p. 106)
1818	George Johnson petitions to inherit Magdalene's land upon her death; petition fails because their parents were not married. (Johnson, 1818)
1831	Margaret Johnson Farley visits Johnson Hall on her way to England. (Johnston 1973, p. 114; Draper Collection, 13F175:75)
1986	Canadian postal stamp issued in Molly Brant's honor.
1994	Molly Brant and Rev. John Stuart added to Anglican Church Calendar. (Diocese of Ontario)

Joseph Brant, at approximately 64 years of age, as depicted in a portrait by Ezra Ames, c. 1806. While reluctant to sit for this piece, Brant felt that this image, of all those done of him over the years, most closely resembled his actual appearance.
Courtesy, New York State Historical Association, Cooperstown, New York (N-421.55).

Appendix 'B'
MOLLY BRANT LETTERS

LETTER FROM MOLLY BRANT TO DANIEL CLAUS

Niagara 23d June
1778

Dear Sir

I have been favor'd with Yours, and the Trunk of parcels by Mr. Street; everything mentioned in the Invoice you sent me has come safe, except the pair of gold Ear rings, which I have not been able to find.

We have a report of Joseph having had a brush with the Rebels, but do not know at what place. A Cayuga Chief is said to be Wounded, one Schohary Indian/Jacob/killed, & one missing since when its reported that Colo Butler, & Joseph have joined; Every hour we look for a confirmation of this news.

I am much obliged to You for the care, & attention in sending me up those very necessary articles; & should be very glad if You have any accounts from New York that You would let me know them, as well as of the health of George & Peggy, whom I hope are agreably settled: My Children are all in good health, & desire their loves to You, Mrs. Claus, Lady & Sir John Johnson. I hope the Time is very near, when we shall all return to our habitations on the Mohawk River.

I am Dr. Sir ever
Affectionately Yours
Mary Brandt

(*Claus Papers,* MG19 F1 2:29, transcribed by Wanda Burch)

LETTER TRANSLATED FROM MARY BRANT'S

LETTER TO COL. CLAUS

dated Carleton Island 12 April 1781

It touches me very sore to hear from Niagara how my younger Brother Joseph Brant was used the 6th of April, by being almost murdered by Col: Johnsons people,[*] what adds to my Grief and Vexation is, that being scarce returned safe from the rebel Country, he must be thus treated by these of the Kings people who always stay quietly at home & in the Fort, while my Brother Continually exposes his Life in going against the Enemy taking prisrs as far as in his power.

For which reason I beg you will speedily let His Excellency General Haldimand hear of it, who alone can heal this Breach of peace & friendship, by his order & reprimand As Commander in Chief.

This usage of my Brother makes me dread the Consequences, as some of the six Nations were Spectators of it, and well remember what Genl. Schuyler told them that they would be ill used and despised by the Kings people for their Services, of which they have now a proof, for which reason I entreat His Excellency General Haldimand to use his Authority and settle this Matter, as it is hard for me to have an only Bror. whom I dearly love to see him thus treated, but what I am most concerned about is that it may affect the Kings Indn. Interest.

The whole Matter is, that the Officers at Niagara are so haughty & proud, not knowing or considering that the Kings Interest is so nearly connected with that of the Indians. Wherefore I beg you will acquaint His Excellency with this, and let me know His Sentiment thereupon—

signed Mary Brant

(*Haldimand Papers,* Add MSS 21774, p. 180)

[* Note: Joseph Brant exhibited unusual behavior and was involved in a drunken brawl on April 6, 1781. Molly Brant's letter to Claus caused him to consult Haldimand who in turn ordered Guy Johnson at Fort Niagara to repair the situation. Indications are that Guy Johnson actually had supported Joseph Brant when the event occurred and that the incident may have been blown out of proportion. Meanwhile, Joseph Brant left Fort Niagara on April 8 for Detroit. (Kelsay, p. 307)]

RECEIPT SIGNED BY MARY BRANT

I acknowledge to have received the sum of Forty four pounds N. York Currency charged in Messrs. Taylor & Forsyths accounts agt. government from & by Order of Colo. Guy Johnson, partly by Cash from himself & the remainder by Forsyth's Bill on Carleton Island, the beginnings of Winter 1780. being for Wampum & other articles which I advanced to Lt. Colo. Butler formerly and which he then acknowledged.

Montreal 11th
October 1782

Present her
Mary wari Brant
Mark

Present
   Simon Clark

I certify that the above is a true Copy of the Origl. recd in my Hand, ready to be produced, but at present kept by me agreeable to an Order of the Department respecting Original Vouchers.

J Johnson

(*Haldimand Papers,* Transcript H1449, Add MSS 21774, p. 111)

A class of Mohawk children, in school at Grand River; engraved by James Peachey. From Daniel Claus's *A Primer for the Use of the Mohawk Children,* **printed in London (1786).** *Courtesy, Metropolitan Toronto Library Board (BR497.4 C47).*

Appendix 'C'
LETTERS FROM PETER JOHNSON

Philadelphia the 18th. November 1773 –

HONORED FATHER,

I am Safely arrived to Mr. Wades in Philadelphia who Seemes to be a Very good man indeed. I had a very good passage from Albany to New York. Left it a friday afternoon with a very Good Company & got to New York a monday Morning where I Dined with Mr. Wallace. & Left that a Tuesday Morning in the Stage Coatch & got to This City Last Night. I like the Place Very well as Yet & hope I Shall much More when I be Settled wrightly to Business. Mr. Chew is going to Set out to Day Back again, that makes me wright in Such a hurry as I have but little time. I Shall write you a Longer Letter by the next Oppertunity as I know but little of the Place Yet — I hope you will write by the next Post & Should be Extremely happy to hear from home. as [soon as] Possible. I Shall write to Mr. Dease this Day & to my Mother & I Shall fould it in Yours — Pray give my Duty & Respects to all Friends at Johnson Hall. Please to Let me know [as to] where I Shall have a good Fiddle as it is a great Deal of Pleasure to Play at Leasure Ours If youl Write to Mr. Wade he will I am Sure get a Very good one in Town. thats all I want at present. I Shall Please God, do all that lies in my P–Power to Please You & all persons here — I Suppose I Shant Stay Long here, for the Sooner I can be Settled the better for me, & I Shall Like it the Better.

I am with great Duty & Respects—

Honoured Sir–
Yours most
Affectionately
P. JOHNSON

INDORSED: [in Sir William's hand]
  Peters Letter from
  Philadelphia–
  Novbr. 1773

(*SWJP*, XII, pp. 1042–43)

Philadelphia 13th. December 1773

HONOUR'D SIR/

I had the pleasure of Seeing Mr. Wallace a few Days ago who Seem'd to be of Opinion I should go to a whole & Retail Shop, and Mr. Wade thinks it better to go to a whole Sale merchant who Deals Largely and import[s] goods from London, & Mr. Wallace also was Speaking of sending me to a gentleman in town who Mr. Wade Seems to Disaprove of & I Believe will Write to you by this post. I Like the place extremely well. Mr. Wade was good enough to Show all the particular places in town to me.

Pray give my Best Duty & Respects to my Mother, Brother & Sister & my Love to Mr. Dease and all friends at Johnson Hall.

I Remain Honoured Sir

> Yours most Dutifully
> & Affectionately
> PETER JOHNSON

Mr. Wade has bought
an Extreme good Violin
for me.–

ADDRESSED:
> To
> The Honble. Sir Willm. Johnson
> at Johnson Hall
> In
> Tryon County

INDORSED: [in Sir William's hand]
> Peters Letter
> Decbr. 13th. 1773

(*SWJP*, VIII, p. 945)

Philada. April 21st.

1774—

HONORED FATHER,

I take the Oppertunity of writing you by Mr. Caldwell a gentleman who Lives in Albany. I am extremely unhappy of not Receiving a Letter from you. & Mr. Dease. I have but a little time to write at present I shall write you a Long Letter by next post I hope My Mother & all are well. we are all expecting to See Doctr. Dease here Soon. which will make me exceeding Joyfull.

We are Just opening our goods at present & are selling as fast as we get them out of the Bales. I expect I shall be very well acquainted with the business in 2 Years — as I can form a pritty near Judgment by what I have Already seen. I can sell almost any kind of Dry goods. I like Mr. Barrell Extremely well. he desirs his Respects to You. As also all our friends here gives there Respective compliments to You. Mr. Wallace is not yet Return'd from Virginia but expect him Soon. I am Sorry I can't write Mr. Dease. I have no more to add but

> Always Remain your
> Most Dutiful Son—
> PETER JOHNSON

Please give my Love to My Mother and all my Affectionate friends—
Please write me by next post.

ADDRESSED:
   To
   Sir William Johnson Bart.
   Johnson Hall
   favd. by Mr. Caldwell   Tryon County

INDORSED: [in Sir William Johnson's hand]
          April 21st. 1774
          My Son Peters letter

(*SWJP*, XIII, pp. 635–36)

Philadelphia April
30th. 1774
HONOR'D SIR,

I take the oppertunity of writing you by Mr. Hare A young Gentleman a Friend of Mr. Wades & Mine — A Clever Geenteel young Man. he is a porter Brewer Lately come from England & has set up a very elegant porter Brewery in this City, & intends takeing a tour to Quebec & Ni[a]gara & them places for his health – with Mr. Allen Son of Judge Allen of this City — Who are both to set off to morrow Morning.

I am Just come from the field where I saw four men hung & a woman the one a Sergant for killing his Wife and the other for Robbing the third for Money makeing the fourth the Brakeing open a house & Robbing also & the fifth a woman for killing her Child. I think its the Most Dismal sight I ever Saw. there were thousands of people altho it rained very hard — it was with the greatest Dificulty I could come near anough to See them, I haer Gouvernour Franklin from the Jerseys is come to town, & that his father has lost his Commission & its thought Gover Franklin will Lose his Gouverment also — I hope the Gentlemen are all well Please to give them my Best Respects

I have wrote to my Mother to Send me some Indian Curiositys As there are Gentlemen & Ladys here very desirous of Seeing them. I would be Glad you would Bring me some french & English Books to read at Leasure hours, & an Indian Book, for I am Afraid I'll lose my Indian Toungue If I dont practice it more than I do.—

I am In great want of a watch as I have to come to dinner, & go early to the Store I dont know what time to go without one. If you'l write Mr. Wade to get me one he will get it very cheap & Good

I am Honor'd father
Your most Dutiful & Affectionate
Son　　PETER JOHNSON

I inclose A Letter
for Betsy in Yours

INDORSED: [in Sir William Johnson's hand]
　　April 30th 1774
　　Letter from Peter
　　at Philadelphia

(*SWJP,* VIII, pp. 1139-40)

Appendix 'D'
TESTIMONY OF A CHILD Of
MOLLY BRANT
(probably Margaret)

England, March 15, 1841

Shortly after My Fathers death My Mother with her family returned to her former residence at Canajoharie My elder Sisters were Sent to School in Schenectady My oldest brother Peter had been previously placed at an Academy in Philadelphia by My Father, at whose decease he was taken home & shortly after left the United States for England with Sir John Johnson Col. Claus Col. Guy Johnson, and Capt. Brant. My Mother Sister of Capt. Brant did not leave the States untill some time after the Revolutionary War Broke out, her wish was to remain on her own property but she was advised by General Herkemer to leave the Country under the representation that her life would be Endangered, She expressed her reluctance to move she had no fears & promised the General that if she remained she should be neutral, that did not Satisfy General Herckimer, he continued sending messages to her if she & her family did not go, they would be taken to Albany jail

The family shortly after this were greatly alarmed one night soon after they had retired, by a loud & continued knocking at the doore, which on being opened several men entered & enquired if Capt. Brant was in the house, to which my Mother replied he was not — they might Search the house if they pleased, which they did, commencing their examination of the sleeping rooms — I was in one of the beds of which they drew back the Curtains, & seeing only Children in it, they declined ferther Search — & withdrew. I perfectly remember my alarm. A few days afterwards, My Mother received a Message informing her that in such a Night stating the time she must be prepared for result as there were persons who would remove her & her family from Canojoharie to Albany — My Mother instantly Sent us to a Neighbour in whome she had confidence — My Mother would not leave her house the Servants were on the watch throughout the Night —

About two O clock in the Morning Several persons were seen on the premises, but no one approached the house — The Servants Who was sent to enquire after us & repeating what had passed occasioned us so great alarm that were put into the utmost confusion having retired we were each Scrambling for our Cloths, The person Who had the care of us sent us out in the adjoining nook where we were screened till My Mother sent for us on the following day, My Mother then determined to leave the Country as she found her residence [in] it was no longer Safe She left her House with reluctance & with a Sore heart taking her Children Seven in Number two black men Servants & two female Servants — we commenced our hurried fatigue & trackless route at night the heardships we encountered in our journing thro' this wilderness to Canada our destination were Countless In our retreet we had to pass within Sight of our own House our hearts ached as we discovered lights through the windows whilst we were stealthily wandering from our home, The Indians who set off with us as our guide Soon left us

(*Hamilton Papers,* Box 1, Folder 12, transcribed by Milton Hamilton from the Draper Manuscripts Collection)

Appendix 'E'
EXTRACTS FROM SIR WILLIAM JOHNSON'S WILL AND LAWYER PETER SILVESTER'S INTERPRETATIONS

And I direct and desire my herein aftermentioned Executors to provide mourning for my House Keeper Mary Brant and for all her Children, also for young Brant & William, both Half bred Mohocks, likewise for my Servants & Slaves. It is also my desire that ye. Sachims of both Mohock Villages be invited to my Funeral, and thereat receive each a black stroud Blancket, Crape and Gloves which they are to wear, and follow as Mourners next & after my own family & friends.

––––––

And First To the Children of my present House Keeper, Mary Brant the Sum of One thousand pounds sterling, viz. to Peter my natural son by said Mary Brant the sum of Three hundred pounds Sterlg. And to each of the rest, being seven in number, One hundred pounds each. The Interest thereof to be duely received, & layed out to the best advantage by their Guardians or Trustees, and also the Income of what other Legacies &ca. as are hereafter to be mentioned, until they come of Age or marry, except what is necessary for their maintenance & Education. Item. To young Brant, alias Kaghneghtago & William, alias Tagawirunta, two Mohawk Lads the sum of One hundred pounds York Curcy. to each, or the Survivor of them.

––––––

I also bequeath to him [Sir John Johnson] all my plate, except a few Articles which I gave to the Children of my House Keeper Mary Brant.

––––––

The other fourth of my Slaves and Stock of Cattle of every kind I give & Bequeath to the Children of Mary Brant my House Keeper, or to the survivors of them, to be divided Equally amongst them Except two Horses, two Cows, two breeding Sows & four Sheep which I would have given (before any Division is made) to Young Brant & William of Conajohare and that within Three months after my Decease. I Also give & devise all my own wearing apparel, of every kind, Woollen, Linen &c. to be equally divided amongst the Children of my said House Keeper Mary Brant share and share alike.

––––––

I Devise & Bequeath unto Peter Johnson my natural Son by Mary Brant, my present Housekeeper, the Farm & Lot of Land which I purchased from the Snells in the Stoneraby Patent with all the Buildings, Mill and other Improvements thereon. Also Two hundred Acres of Land adjoining thereto, being part of Kingsborough patent to be laid out in a compact body between the Garoge & Caniadutta Creeks. Also four thousand Acres in the Royal Grant, now called Kingsland next to the Mohawk River, and another Stripe or piece of Land in the Royal Grant from the Little Falls or carrying place to Lot No. one, almost opposite the house of Hannicol Herkimer, & includes two Lots No. Three & No. Two along the river side, and wh. are now occupied by Ury House &c.

I Divise & Bequeath unto Elizabeth Sister of the aforesaid Peter & Daughter of Mary Brant, All that Farm & Lot of Land in Harrison's Patent on the north side of the Mohawk River No. Nineteen, Containing near Seven hundred Acres, bought by me several years ago of Mr. Brown of Salem, with all the buildings & appurtenances thereunto belonging. Also Two thousand Acres of Land in the Royal Grant, now called Kingsland & that to be layed out Joining to that of her brother Peter, both which she & the Heirs of her body lawfully begotten are to Enjoy peaceably &quietly forever.

To Magdalene Sister of the two former & Daughter of Mary Brant I divise & bequeath the Farm near to Antony's Nose No. Eight, Containing about nine hundred Acres of Land, & on which Mr. Brat [Bratt] now lives, with all the buildings, Improvements and other appurtenances thereunto belonging. Also Two thousand Acres of Land in the Royal Grant now called Kingsland, adjoining to that Tract of her Sister Elizabeth.

To Margaret, Sister of the above named Magdalene & Daughter of Mary Brant I Devise & Bequeath two Lots of Land, part of Stoneraby Patent, The one viz. No. Twenty five which I bought of William Markell contains one hundred acres, the other number Twelve contains One hundred & thirty one Acres & a half or thereabouts, which I purchased from Peter Weaver. Also two thousand Acres of Land in the Royal Grant now called Kingsland, to be laid out for her next to that of her Sister Magdalene.

To George my natural son by Mary Brant & brother to the four before mentioned Children I Devise & Bequeath Two Lots of Land part of Sacondaga patent known by No. Forty three & Forty four & called New Philadelphia containing Two hundred & fifty Acres each; Also a small Patent or Tract of Land called John Brackans, lying on the North side of ye. Mohawk River, almost opposite to the Canajoharie Castle & contains Two hundred & Eighty Acres of thereabouts, & Lastly Three Thousand Acres in the Royal Grant now called Kingsland next to the Two thousand Acres given to his Sister Margaret. The said Farms & Tracts of Land with all the Buildings & other appurtenances belonging to them, are to be by him & the Heirs of his body lawfully begotten forever quietly & peaceably possessed & Enjoyed.

To Mary, daughter of Mary Brant & Sister of the before mentioned Five Children I divise & Bequeath Two thousand Acres of Land in the Royal Grant now called Kingsland, adjoining to them of her brother George. Also two Lots in Stoneraby Patent No. Thirty Six & Thirty Eight containing about One Hundred & fifty Acres, which I bought of Peter Davis & Hannis Kitts.

To Susanna, Daughter of Mary Brant & Sister of the foregoing Six Children, I Devise & bequeath Three thousand Acres of the Royal Grant now called Kingsland to be laid out adjoining to them of her Sister Mary.

To Anne, Sister of the foregoing seven Children by Mary Brant I Devise & Bequeath Three Thousand Acres of the Royal Grant now called Kingsland, to be laid out next to that of her Sister Susannah, And to be by her & the Heirs of her body lawfully begotten, forever quietly & peaceably possessed & enjoyed.

To Young Brant, alias Kaghnechtago [Kaghnaghtago] of Canojohare I give & bequeath One thousand Acres of Land in the Royal Grant now called Kingsland to be layed out next to & adjoining the before mentioned Land of Anne Daughter of Mary Brant. Also to William alias Tagawirunte of Canajohare. One thousand Acres of Land in said Royal Grant, alias Kingsland, adjoining that of Brants, to be by them & the Heirs of their bodys lawfully begotten forever quietly & peaceably possessed & enjoyed.

It is also my Will & desire, that in case any of the before mentioned Eight Children of mine by Mary Brant, should dye without Issue their Share or Shares as well as my personal as Real Estate, be equally divided amongst the Survivors of them by their Guardians.

To my prudent & faithfull Housekeeper Mary Brant, mother of the before mentioned Eight children, I will and bequeath the Lot No. one being part of the Royal Grant now called Kingsland, and is opposite to the Land whereon Hannicol Herkimer now lives, which she is to enjoy peaceably during her natural life, after which it is to be possessed by her Son Peter & his Heirs forever. I also give & bequeath to my said Housekeeper One Negroe Wench named Jenny the Sister of Juba, also the sum of Two hundred pounds current money of N. York to be paid to her by my Executors within three months after my decease.

————

... it is also my Will & Desire that John Butler, Jelles Fonda, John Dease, James Stevenson, Henry Frey [Fry] & Joseph Chew Esqrs. be and act as Guardians or Trustees of my before mentioned Eight Children by Mary Brant my present Housekeeper in full confidence that (from the close connection of the former, and the long uninterrupted friendship subsisting between me & the latter,) they will strictly and as Brothers inviolably observe and Execute this my last charge to them. The Strong dependence on, & expectation of which unburthens my mind, allays my cares, & makes a change the less alarming.

(*SWJP,* XII, pp. 1062–76)

LEGAL OPINIONS OF PETER SILVESTER

1st. August 1774

Points arising & Questions proposed upon Sir William Johnson's Barts. Will dated the 27th January 1774

I Give & bequeath to the Persons therein mend. the Sum of Money in the said Will mentioned to be Paid them by my Executors *out of the money which I may have in the Three pr Cent Consolidated Annuities &c*

Question 1st. How is this money to be got out of the ffunds, or Received, or Recovered of the Agent in England?

Answer I am of Opinion that the Probate of the Will from the Prerogative Office of this Province will not be Sufficient to enable a Recovery of this money at Home, but that Letters of Administration must be obtained in England in Case of any Scruples in Paying it.

Question 2d. What is to be done with the One Thousand Pounds Sterling divised to the Children of Mary Brant?

Answer 2d. I think it may with Safety be paid to the Trustees (upon a Presumption that there is a Sufficiency of Personal Estate to Satisfy all Debts & Legacies) proper Releases and Acquittances Shou'd be taken on the Payment of this Sum, and I would Recommend it also in every other matter.

Question 3d. The one fourth Part of all his Slaves he gives to his Son John Johnson, and the same of his Stock of Cattle of every kind. To his two Daughters Ann Claus and Mary Johnson two ffourths of his Slaves & Stock of Cattle; The other ffourth of his Slaves and Stock of Cattle of every kind, Sir William gives, and bequeaths to the Children of Mary Brant his Housekeeper, or to the Survivors of them to be divided equally amongst them, except two Horses, — two Cows, two Breeding Sows, and four Sheep which I would have given (before any Division is made) to young *Brant* and William of Canajoharie, Is the Clause of Exception, vize. the two Horses &c to be taken out of the whole of this Bequest, or any other, and what Part.

Answer I think they must be taken out of the last ffourth.

Case &
Questn. 4th. I Devise & bequeath unto Peter Johnson the ffarm & Lot of land which I purchased from the Snells in the Stonearaby Patent &c also two Hundred acres of Land adjoining thereto, —Also ffour thousand Acres in the Royal Grant, and another

Stripe or Piece of land in the Royal Grant from the little ffals &c

Answer 4th   I am of Opinion that, only an Estate for life is Devised by the above Clauses.

Question 5th. What Estate has Magdalene to the ffarm at Antony's Nose No. 8 containing about 900 Acres.

Answer 5th.   I think it only an Estate for Life.

Quest. 6th   What Estate has Margaret to the two Lots of Land part of Stoneraby Patent, the one viz. No. 25. & 12. Also the two thousd. acres of the Royal Grant.

Answer 6th   I think this also an Estate for life only

Questn. 7th   What Estate has Mary Daughter of Mary Brant in the two thousd. Acres of land &c devised to her?

Answer 7th.   Only an Estate for Life, I think.

Question 8th   What Estate has Susanna in the Three thousand acres of the Royal Grant?

Ansr. 8th   I think that She likewise has only an Estate for life.

Questn. 9th.   What is Chattles, or the Personal Estate, and as such to be put on the Inventory.

Answer 9th.   They are Divided into Real, and Personal, — Real such as Leases for life, Years &c. — Personal — such as Cash, Bonds, Book Debts, everything moveable — Grain Standing & growing or severed.

Questn. 10th   What is to become of such of the Real Estate as is not taken Notice of, or Divided by the Will.

Answer 10th   Sir John will be Intitled to it as Heir at Law.

Quest. 11th.   Who is Intitled to such Part of the Personal Estate as is not particularly bequeathed by the Will?

Answer 11th   It must be Divided equally between Sir John, and his Sisters agreeable to the Statute of Distribution, as if there had been no will.

P. Silvester

NB The aforegoing is a Cursory Opinion. P.S:

(*SWJP*, VIII, pp. 1189–90)

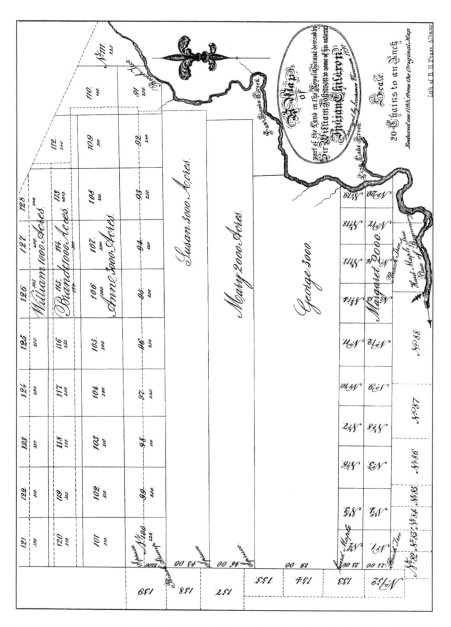

This property survey, detailing a portion of the Kingsland land plan, shows part of the "Royal Grant devised by Sir William Johnson to some of his natural Indian Children." This survey was done by Laurence Vrooman in 1797 (long after the lands had been seized during the Revolution), to show what the actual Kingsland division would have been. Lithograph by R.H. Pease, Albany. From O'Callaghan's *Documentary History Of New York.*

Appendix 'F'
JOSEPH CHEW'S MEMORIALS
ON BEHALF OF THE CHILDREN

To the Commissioners Appointed by Act of Parliament to Enquire into the Losses and Services of the American Loyalists

The Memorial of Joseph Chew Guardian of the Persons and Estates of Elizabeth, Magadalen, Margaret, George, Mary, Susana & Ann, Infant Children of Mrs. Mary Brant, being Thereunto Appointed by the Last Will and Testiment of the Late Sir Wm. Johnson Bart. of Tryon County and Province of New York

Shewith
    that Mrs. Brant from her Connection with the Family of the Late Sir Wm. Johnson, her Zeal and Endeavours in Persuading the Indian Nations with whom she had great Interest in Continuing firm to the Royal Cause, became first an Object of the Jealousy of the Leaders of the Rebellion as Obliged her from after Sir John Johnson was forced from the Country in 1776. to quit her Habbitation & Property at Canajoharie on the Mohawk River, Tryon County, and Retire to His Majesty's Fort at Niagara with her small Children Leaving all the Estates and Property of the Said Children which were taken Possession of by Committees and Persons in Rebellion, and are now held by them.
    Your Memorialist at the Time Mrs. Brant and her Children Left the County was doing duty with His Majesty's Army in the District of new York he Therefore at Present is not able to Say What Personal Property the Children Lost, their Right and Titles in the Real Estates maintained in the Schedule herewithin delivered will appear by the Last Will of Sir William Johnson Bart. Registered in London a Copy of which is in his Possession.
    Your Memorialist therefore Prays the Case of these Orphan Children may be taken into Consideration that under your Report they may receive such aid and Relief on Their Losses Shall be found to Merit.

                                                         Joseph Chew

London 13 March 1786

Proof, the Will of Sir William Johnson Bart. and which is in my hand.

To the Commissioners Appointed by Act of Parliament for Enquiring into the losses and services of the American Loyalists

The Memorial of Joseph Chew in behalf of the Children of Mrs. Mary Brant

Representing
    That being appointed a guardian for the said Children by the Last Will and Testament of Sir William Johnson Bart. Deced. he did on the 25 of March 1784 Lodge a Memorial in the Office for American Claims Praying the loses these Children had Suffered by theAmerican Rebellion might be taken into just Consideration, a Copy of which memorial and the Schedule he then delivered is hereunto assured
    That about the Time of the Commissioners going to Nova Scotia he had some hopes from the Promises made to the Friends of these Children by Mr. Clinton the Present Governor of New York that a stop would be put to the Sales of their Estates, and Converted in the Memorial he had Lodged being sent to American for an Enquiry. Since which he is informed that the Committees of the Late County of Tryon or the Commissioners of that District have Continued to Sell and dispose of those Estates, that he thinks he has good Authority to say, and believes it will also appear to you, that no Part Thereof will Ever be Restored to the Said Children.
    Your Memorialist also begs Leave to add That two others of their Guardians are now in London as are Several Witnesses whose Testimony will Enable him to Prove the Value of there Estates, That in Justice to the Claimands as well as in the discharge of his Duty. He Humbly Prays an Investigation of those Claims may take Place here, in order to Perpetuate the Testimony of Such Witnesses on the Examination, and further he makes this application at the Particular Request of Capt. Brant a Chief of the united Indian Nations Uncle to those Children.
    Upon these Principles your memorialist Prays a day for such hearing may be appointed before the Evidence now has quit the Kingdom.

    Frith Street Soho No. 18
    15th March 1786

(Great Britain, Public Record Office, Audit Office 13, Vol. 11[2]-12[1])

Appendix 'G'
ETHAN ALLEN'S DESCRIPTION
OF HIS CAPTURE BY
PETER JOHNSON

... being almost entirely surrounded but with such vast unequal numbers, I ordered a retreat, but found that those of the enemy, who were of the country, and their Indians, could run as fast as my men, though the regulars could not. Thus I retreated near a mile, and some of the enemy, with the savages, kept flanking me, and others crowded hard in the rear: in fine I expected in a very short time, to try the world of spirits; for I was apprehensive that no quarter would be given to me, and therefore had determined to sell my life as dear as I could. One of the enemy's officers boldly pressing in the rear, discharged his fusee at me; the ball whistled near me, as did many others that day. I returned the salute, and missed him, as running had put us both out of breath; for I conclude we were not frightened, I then saluted him with my tongue in a harsh manner, and told him that inasmuch as his numbers were so far superior to mine, I would surrender, provided I could be treated with honor, and be assured of good quarter for myself and the men who were with me, and he answered I should; another officer coming up directly after, confirmed the treaty; upon which I agreed to surrender with my party, which then consisted of thirty–one effective men, and seven wounded. I ordered them to ground their arms, which they did.

The officer I capitulated with, then directed me and my party to advance towards him, which was done, I handed him my sword, and in half a minute after a savage, part of whose head was shaved, being almost naked and painted, with feathers intermixed with the hair of the other side of his head, came running to me with an incredible swiftness; he seemed to advance with more than mortal speed (as he approached near me, his hellish visage was beyond all description, snakes eyes appear innocent in comparison of his, his features extorted, malice, death, murder, and the wrath of devils and damned spirits are the emblems of his countenance) and in less than twelve feet of me, presented his firelock; at the instant, of his present, I twitched the officer to whom I gave my sword, between me and the savage, but he flew round with great fury, trying to single me out to shoot me without killing the officer; but by this time I was near as nimble as he, keeping the officer in such a position that his danger was my defence, but in less than half a minute, I was attacked by just such another imp of hell;

then I made the officer fly around with incredibly velocity, for a few seconds of time, when I perceived a Canadian (who had lost one eye, as appeared afterwards) taking my part against the savages; and in an instant an Irishman came to my assistance with a fixed bayonet, and drove away the fiends, swearing by Jasus he would kill them. This tragic scene composed my mind. The escaping from so awful a death, made even imprisonment happy, the more so as my conquerors on the field treated me with great civility and politeness.

(Allen, pp. 19–22)

Appendix 'H'
BRIEF BIOGRAPHIES OF PEOPLE IN MOLLY BRANT'S LIFE

• *Joseph Brant (Thayendanegea)* •

Molly's brother was born in 1743. At the age of thirteen, he accompanied William Johnson to Lake George in the 1755 campaign. He was educated at Wheelock's School and served as interpreter for Johnson's Indian Department. A devout Anglican, Brant helped Reverend John Stuart translate religious texts into Mohawk. Appointed Secretary to Guy Johnson in 1774, Brant went to England with the Loyalist delegation at the outbreak of the American Revolution. There he was presented at court and had his portrait painted by Romney. Returning to America, Brant fought for the Loyalist cause, leading his Indian troops on numerous raids on the frontier, including the Battle of Oriskany. After the war, in cooperation with Sir John Johnson, Superintendent of Indian Affairs, he secured a large land grant along the Grand River of present-day Ontario where he helped many of his adherents settle. This land was formally granted in 1784 by General Haldimand, in the name of the Crown. It encompassed some 786,000 acres, to be reserved for the Mohawk and others of the Six Nations. He died in Canada on November 24, 1807.

• *John Butler* •

Butler was born in Connecticut in 1728, son of a military captain who moved his family to the Mohawk Valley in 1742. His father, Walter, was commandant of Fort Hunter and Oswego for many years. John Butler was commissioned captain and served in the Crown Point campaign of 1757, at Ticonderoga in 1758 and at Niagara with Sir William Johnson in 1759, becoming leader of the Indian allies during the siege. He was a trusted agent of Sir William in the conduct of Indian affairs and was appointed by him as one of the guardians of Molly Brant's children.

John Butler and his son, Walter, went to Canada with Guy Johnson and Daniel Claus in 1775. Butler was stationed at Niagara as deputy Indian commissioner with instructions to preserve the good will of the Iroquois. He participated in the Battle of Oriskany, after which he began recruiting a battalion of rangers which he commanded, first as major, then as lieutenant-colonel. "Butler's Rangers" raided the frontiers of New York and Pennsylvania during the American Revolution and opposed Sullivan in 1779. After the war, he received land and compensation for his losses and served as commissioner of Indian Affairs at Niagara. He died there, at Newark (Niagara-on-the-Lake, Ontario), on May 13, 1796.

• *Joseph Chew* •

Joseph Chew was a descendant of an old Virginia family and one of Sir William Johnson's closest confidants. An officer in King George's War which ended in 1748, Chew went to Connecticut where he was rescued from bankruptcy by Johnson. Returning to New York, Chew became one of Sir William's tenants, living close to Johnson Hall on land which Johnson eventually left to him in his will. After returning to New York and Johnson's patronage, Chew's fortunes rapidly changed. He was appointed by Johnson as Justice of the Peace, highway commissioner and an official of the local courts. He was one of the executors of Sir William's will and one of the guardians for the children, a charge he took seriously as he pursued their Loyalist claims to a successful conclusion.

After Sir William's death, Chew was appointed Secretary of Indian Affairs by Guy Johnson, a post which he also held in Canada in the 1790s. In 1796, upon hearing of Molly Brant's death, Chew wrote, "my old friend Molly Brant died lately at Kingston." (Burton, p. 449)

• *Daniel Claus* •

Born in 1727 in Germany, Claus emigrated to Philadelphia where he joined Conrad Weiser on a trip into the Mohawk Valley in 1749. There he met William Johnson and became one of his protégés. After living with the Mohawk to learn their language and ways, Claus was hired by Johnson as a member of his Indian Department. Claus served in many roles, both military and diplomatic, and was stationed in Montreal as Johnson's agent. After marrying Sir William's and Catherine Weissenberg's daughter, Ann (Nancy), on April 13, 1762, Claus established his own home on the Mohawk River four hundred yards from Guy Johnson's house.

Claus was famous for his musical abilities; one visitor described staying at Claus' home, Williamsburg, and spending the entire time playing music with him. Others also reported that Claus had running water in his kitchen and a spouting fountain in his garden. Claus joined Guy Johnson when the latter left for Canada and served as an Indian agent and diplomat throughout the war. His voluminous papers, now in the National Archives of Canada in Ottawa, contain valuable, lucid accounts of his activities and of the people he knew, including Molly Brant. Claus's first journal, kept upon his arrival in America and written in German, has recently been translated, heavily annotated, and published by the American Philosophical Society. After the war, Claus lived in England. He died in Cardiff, Wales, in 1787. His wife died eleven years later. Their son, William Claus, fought with British forces in Canada during the War of 1812, serving as lieutenant-colonel of the 1st Lincoln Regiment.

• *Dr. John Dease* •

John Dease was born in Ireland about 1745, the son of Sir William Johnson's sister, Anne. He emigrated to America and became his uncle's personal physician during Sir William's last years. While living at Johnson Hall, he also was a special companion to young Peter Johnson. Dease was left a generous inheritance by Sir William and was appointed both as one of the executors of the will and as one of the guardians for the children. He went to Canada with Guy Johnson where he was active on the Loyalist side. He was present in Montreal when Peter Johnson helped capture Ethan Allen. Dease and his wife had five sons, one of whom became a doctor serving at Fort Vancouver in Oregon for the Hudsons Bay Company. John Dease died in Canada, in 1801.

• *Malcolm Fraser•*

Born in Scotland in 1733, Malcolm Fraser died in Murray Bay, Lower Canada, in 1815. He was serving with the 78th Regiment of Foot by 1757 and was with Wolfe at Louisbourg, in 1758, and at Quebec, in 1759. He married Marie Allaire about 1760 and in 1761 acquired a seigneury at Mt. Murray at Murray Bay, Quebec. He retired at half–pay in 1763. Fraser became captain and quartermaster in the 1st Battalion, Royal Highland Emigrants during the Revolutionary War and was stationed mostly in Montreal, Carleton Island and Richelieu. He was discharged in June 1784 and again put on half–pay.

• *Sir Frederick Haldimand* •

Haldimand was born in Switzerland and served in the Dutch army before joining the British forces during the Seven Years War. He distinguished himself in the attack against Ticonderoga in July 1758 and in the defense of Oswego in 1759. He was later lieutenant-general and colonel of the 60th (Royal American) Regiment of Foot and succeeded Sir Guy Carleton as governor and commander in chief of Canada in 1778. He returned to England in November 1784 and died in Switzerland in 1791.

• *Brant Johnson (Kaghneghtago)* •

Brant Johnson, the eldest of William Johnson's two Mohawk sons, prior to those with Molly Brant, was born in the 1740s and lived at Canajoharie. In July 1765 he married a white woman, a captive returned by the western Indians the previous fall. The wedding was performed by missionary Theophilus Chamberlain who described the event. Also married in the same ceremony were Joseph Brant and his first wife. Brant Johnson's wife could speak several Indian languages, and the couple settled at Canajoharie until forced to go to Canada. Brant Johnson was left a legacy of land and goods in Sir William Johnson's will.

Living at Niagara during the winter of 1779–80 along with Molly Brant and other old friends, Brant Johnson served in Butler's Rangers as a scout. His daughters, one of whom was described by Claus as "a genius," were schooled with their cousins in Montreal. The family received compensation for their losses after the war. One daughter married Alexander Stewart, a lawyer who assisted Joseph Brant in much of his legal business. Another daughter may have married an Agnew and moved to Ohio. Kaghneghtago's date of death is not known.

• Guy Johnson •

Another nephew of Sir William, Guy Johnson was born in Ireland about 1740. He came to America to assist his famous uncle. Guy Johnson served with American provincial troops against the French in 1757 and commanded a company of rangers under Amherst in the 1759 and 1760 campaigns. He married Sir William's and Catherine Weissenberg's youngest daughter, Mary (Polly), in 1763, and was his assistant in the Indian Department. Guy succeeded his uncle as superintendent in 1774. After the outbreak of the American Revolution in 1775, he realized he could not return to his Mohawk Valley home. He departed in May of that year for Oswego, where he arranged a significant Indian conference. His wife died there on July 11th. From Oswego, Guy, his two young daughters, and many of his friends left for Montreal. Johnson was associated with Joseph Brant and the Mohawk in their fighting against the Americans during the 1779 Sullivan campaign. In 1783, following a scandal and a court case about the expenses of the Indian Department, Haldimand replaced Guy as Indian Commissioner with Sir John Johnson. After going to London to make his claims against the government, Guy Johnson died in poverty on March 5, 1788.

• Sir John Johnson •

Son, by Catherine Weissenberg, and heir of Sir William Johnson, John was born on November 5, 1742. After attending an academy in Philadelphia in 1759, he was captain of a company of the New York militia by 1760 and served in the campaign to suppress Pontiac's Rebellion. John Johnson attended many Indian conferences with his father and was commissioned colonel of a regiment of horse in the New York militia. In 1765 he accompanied Lord Adam Gordon to England where Johnson was knighted by the King. On June 30, 1773, he married Mary Watts, daughter of a prominent New York family, and they made their home at Fort Johnson. He succeeded to his father's baronetcy and a large part of his great estates upon Sir William's death in July 1774.

John Johnson fled with a band of followers to Canada in May 1776, where he was commissioned lieutenant-colonel and authorized to raise the King's Royal Regiment of New York, a unit that became commonly known as the "Royal Greens." Johnson participated in the Battle of Oriskany and in many raids into western New York. He was made Indian Commissioner and served in that capacity for many years overseeing the affairs of the Iroquois and helping to settle the Loyalists, many of whom had been his followers. Large land grants and a sum of money were rewarded to him in compensation for his losses. Johnson died in Montreal on January 4, 1830.

• William Johnson of Canajoharie (Tagawirunte) •

Born in the 1750s and raised by his mother's family at Canajoharie, Sir William's son was known for his violent temper and may have experienced some conflict over his roles in life. His father sent him to Wheelock's School where young William proved troublesome. Sir William instructed Wheelock to send him back if he persisted in his behavior even after being "used with severity." The following year, 1767, Tagawirunte was sent to Thomas Barton in Lancaster, Pennsylvania for schooling. There he stayed eight months learning arithmetic, reading and writing so successfully that Barton thought he could become Sir William's secretary, or at least be able to teach in one of the Indian schools. In Lancaster, Barton had some difficulty persuading William to cease challenging many of the German boys in the neighborhood to fight but reported that his family all were fond of him. However, with the outbreak of Indian troubles in the spring of 1768, William became "dissatisfied, sullen, careless" and demanded to return home. He left with his books and moved back to Canajoharie.

When the Revolutionary War broke out, William joined Guy Johnson in 1775 for the trip to Canada. After the battle at St. John's, he returned to Canajoharie where he threatened the local rebels and finally killed a man in a tavern brawl. Returning again to Canada, he subsequently served with Joseph Brant's forces, and was an emissary for Butler to Samuel Kirkland. Reportedly killed at Oriskany, he apparently was still alive in 1779, and, by family tradition, was involved in a military incident in the early 1790s which crippled him for life. He had died by 1795. In May of that year, his son, Moses, conducted a land transaction. The indenture was between Moses Johnson, eldest son and heir of William, alias Tagawirunte, and Douw Fonda and was for land in Kingsland, part of William Johnson's inheritance from his father. Since Moses was named as "eldest son," William must have fathered more than one.

• *Judge Thomas Jones* •

Jones was born April 30, 1731 at Fort Neck, South Oyster Bay, Long Island, the son of the Justice of the Supreme Court of New York Colony. Thomas succeeded his father to that post in 1773 after a successful law career. He presided over the last court under the Crown held at White Plains in 1776. By June of that year, he was under house arrest on Long Island. Jones spent most of the war in that situation at his Long Island estate, and began writing his memoirs, which contain information about his visits to Johnson Hall. His eventual manuscript, *History of New York During the Revolutionary War, and of The Leading Events in the Other Colonies at that Period,* (believed to have been authored between 1783 and 1788) is a history of the American Revolution written from a Loyalist perspective. In 1779, he was kidnapped and transported to Connecticut where he was held in exchange for General Gold Sellick Silliman. In 1781, he and his wife, Anne de Lancey Jones, sailed to England. Under the New York Act of Attainder, which became effective upon the implementation of the peace treaty in 1783, he was forbidden to return to the United States under pain of death. By name, Jones' life was declared *ipso facto forfeited,* and his estates confiscated. He died in England on July 25, 1792.

• Samuel Kirkland •

Kirkland was born November 20, 1741 in Connecticut, the son of a minister. He attended Wheelock's School where he became a friend of Joseph Brant and other Mohawk. Samuel Kirkland graduated from the College of New Jersey in 1765 *in absentia* since he already had gone to serve as a missionary amongst the Iroquois. Ordained in Lebanon, Connecticut in 1766, he decided to make his permanent mission among the Oneida. Kirkland worked in that capacity for forty years. He married a niece of Wheelock's and took her to the Oneida mission in 1769. During the American Revolution, many Oneida aided the American cause while Kirkland directed Oneida scouts, and served as chaplain at Fort Stanwix and with the Sullivan expedition. Following the war, he assisted the Americans with their negotiations with the Iroquois, and he resumed his mission. Kirkland obtained a charter in 1793 for Hamilton Oneida Academy, the institution now known as Hamilton College. He died on February 28, 1808.

• Reverend John Stuart •

John Stuart was born in Pennsylvania in 1740. He became a school teacher in Lancaster before being ordained an Anglican priest in London in 1770. Returning to America that year, he became missionary to the Mohawk at Fort Hunter and was soon a close friend of Sir William Johnson, Molly Brant, and Joseph Brant. By 1772, Joseph Brant was assisting Stuart in translating the Anglican prayer book and parts of the Bible into Mohawk.

Placed under house arrest at the beginning of the American Revolution, Stuart and his family eventually were exchanged and allowed to go to Canada. There he founded the first English school in Montreal and was chaplain to the King's Royal Regiment of New York. After the war, he founded the first Anglican church in Kingston with the help of old friends like Molly Brant. From Kingston, Stuart traveled frequently to the Mohawk settlements to perform religious ceremonies for them. When Kingston became the capital of Upper Canada, Stuart was appointed chaplain to the Legislative Council and later offered a judgeship, which he refused. He died in 1811 and was buried at St. George's (now St Paul's) Church, in the same burying ground where Molly Brant and many members of her family are interred.

• BIBLIOGRAPHY •
Commonly Used Abbreviations

DHNY   O' Callaghan, *Documentary History of the State of New York*
DRCHSNY   O' Callaghan and Fernow, *Documents Relative to the Colonial History of the State of New York*
SWJP   Sullivan *et al., The Papers of Sir William Johnson*

• • • • • • • • • • • • •

Allen, Ethan. *The Narrative of Colonel Ethan Allen.* (New York: Corinth Books, 1961). Based on the 1930 edition by the Fort Ticonderoga Museum.

Army List. (London, 1776-1778).

Axtell, James (ed.). *The Indian Peoples of Eastern America: A Documentary History of the Sexes.* (New York: Oxford University Press, 1981).

Axtell, James (ed.). *The Invasion Within: The Contest of Cultures in Colonial North America.* (New York: Oxford University Press, 1985).

Bataille, Gretchen M., and Sands, Kathleen Mullen (eds.). *American Indian Women Telling Their Lives.* (Lincoln: University of Nebraska Press, 1984).

Bonvillain, Nancy, "Iroquoian Women," in Bonvillain, Nancy (ed.), *Studies on Iroquoian Culture.* Occasional publications in Northeastern Anthropology, No. 6. (Rindge, New Hampshire: Franklin Pierce College, 1980), pp. 47-58.

Brant Family Papers. National Archives of Canada, Ottawa, M619 F6, 1:1-213.

Burch, Wanda. "Sir William Johnson and Eighteenth–Century Medicine in the New York Colony," in Peter Benes (ed.), *Medicine and Health, The Annual Proceedings of the Dublin Seminar for New England Folklife.* (Boston: Boston University, 1990), pp. 55–65.

Burch, Wanda. "Sir William Johnson's Cabinet of Curiosities," *New York History,* LXXI, No. 3 (July 1990), pp. 261–82.

Burleigh, H.C. *Deforests and Avesnes and Kast, McGinness,* published typescript ([N.p.1977?]) in Special Collections, James A. Gibson Library, Brock University, St. Catharines, Ontario.

Burton, M. Agnes (ed). *Historical Collections: Collections and Researches Made by the Michigan Pioneer and Historical Society,* Vol. XX, 1912, p. 449.

Butterfield, L.H (ed). *Adams Family Correspondence.* (2 vols.; New York: Atheneum Publications, 1965).

Campbell Family Papers. The New York State Library, Albany, 23 boxes, #EP10062.

Campbell, Marjorie Freeman. *Niagara, Hinge of the Golden Arc.* (Toronto: The Ryerson Press, 1958).

Campbell, Patrick. *Travels in the Interior Inhabited Parts of North America in the Years 1791 and 1792.* Edited by H.H. Langton. (Toronto: The Champlain Society, 1937).

Campbell, William W. *Annals of Tryon County; Or, the Border Wars of New–York, During the Revolution.* (New York: J. & J. Harper, 1831).

Cataraqui Archaeological Research Foundation. *Rideaucrest Development Property Mitigation Bb Gc-19.* (Kingston, Ontario: December 1989).

Chew, Joseph. "The Memorial of Joseph Chew Guardian of the Persons and Estates of the Children of Sir William Johnson as written to the Commissioners Appointed to Enquire into the Losses and Services of the American Loyalists". Transcribed from microfilm copy provided by Public Record Office, Audit Office 13, Vol. 11[2] - 12[1], London.

Claus Papers. National Archives of Canada, Ottawa.

Clinton, George. *Public Papers of George Clinton, First Governor of New York, 1777-1795-1801-1804.* (10 vols.; Albany: The State of New York, 1899-1914).

Colden, Cadwallader. *The History of the Five Indian Nations of Canada.* (2 vols.; Toronto: George N. Morang & Company, Ltd., 1902).

The Compact Edition of the Oxford English Dictionary. (2 vols.; Glasgow: Oxford University Press, 1971).

Cruickshank, Helen Gere (ed.). *John and William Bartram's America.* (Garden City, New York: Doubleday & Company, Inc., 1961).

De Forest, L. Effingham (ed.). "Hannah Lawrence Schieffelin's Letter", *The New York Genealogical and Biographical Record,* LXXII, No. 2 (1941), pp. 120–23.

De Lancey, Edward Floyd (ed.). *History of New York During the Revolutionary War, and of the Leading Events In the Other Colonies at That Period, by Thomas Jones.* (2 vols.; New York: The New-York Historical Society, 1879).

Dictionary of Canadian Biography. (12 vols and Index; Toronto: University of Toronto Press, 1966-1991).

Diocese of Ontario, Anglican. *The Cathedral Church of St. George.* (Kingston, Ontario: Diocese of Ontario, 1989).

Draper Collection, Brant Manuscripts. State Historical Society of Wisconsin, Madison. Microfilm copies available at The New York State Library, Albany.

Dunne, James F. and McCaffery, Lucy. "O'Cahan, The Blind Harper of Johnson Hall," *Folk Harp Journal,* No. 47 (December 1984).

Dunnigan, Brian Leigh. *Siege—1759: The Campaign Against Niagara.* (Youngstown, New York: Old Fort Niagara Association, 1996).

Elmer, Ebenezer. "Journal Kept During an Expedition to Canada in 1776," *New Jersey Historical Society Proceedings* No. 2 (1847), pp. 95–146, 150–94; No. 3 (1848), pp. 21–56, 90–102; No. 10 (1925), pp. 410–24.

Ferguson, John. The Memorial of John Ferguson, "Petitions for Grants of Land in Upper Canada, Second Series, 1796-99." With an introduction and notes by E. A. Cruikshank, *Ontario Historical Society Papers and Records,* XXVI. (Toronto: 1930).

File, Celia. *The Children of Molly Brant,* 1933. Typescript of research on file at Johnson Hall State Historic Site, Johnstown, New York.

Fraser, Alexander (ed.). *Second Report of the Bureau of Archives for the Province of Ontario.* (Toronto: L.K. Cameron, 1905).

Grant, Anne. *Memoirs of an American Lady: With Sketches of Manners and Scenes in America, as They Existed Previous to the Revolution.* (Albany: J. Munsell, 1876).

Graymont, Barbara. *The Iroquois in the American Revolution.* (Syracuse, New York: Syracuse University Press, 1972).

Graymont, Barbara. "Konwatsi?tsiaiénni" In *Dictionary of Canadian Biography,* IV (1979), pp. 416–19.

Green, Gretchen. "Molly Brant, Catharine Brant, and Their Daughters: A Study in Colonial Acculturation," *Ontario History,* LXXXI, No. 3 (September 1989), pp. 235–50.

Guldenzopf, David B. "The Colonial Transformation of Mohawk Iroquois Society." Unpublished Ph.D. dissertation, Department of Anthropology, State University of New York at Albany, 1986. (Ann Arbor, Michigan, University Microfilms).

Gundry, Eldon P. "William Lamb of Delaware County, New York, and His Descendants." Copy in Flint, Michigan Public Library, 1957.

Gundy, H. Pearson. "Molly Brant – Loyalist," *Ontario History,* LIV, No. 3 (Summer 1953), pp. 97–108.

Guzzardo, John Christopher. "Sir William Johnson's Official Family: Patron and Clients in an Anglo–American Empire, 1742–1777." Unpublished Ph.D. dissertation, Department of History, Syracuse University, 1975. (Ann Arbor, Michigan, University Microfilms).

Frederick Haldimand Papers, British Library, London, England. Microfilm copies in the National Archives of Canada, Ottawa, Ontario.

Halsey, Francis W. (ed.). *A Tour of Four Great Rivers: the Hudson, Mohawk, Susquehanna and Delaware in 1769, Being the Journal of Richard Smith of Burlington, New Jersey.* (Port Washington, New York: Ira J. Friedman, Inc., 1964).

Hamilton, Milton W. "The Diary of the Reverend John Ogilvie, 1750-1759," *The Bulletin of the Fort Ticonderoga Museum,* X, No. 5 (February 1961), pp. 331-85.

Hamilton, Milton W. *Sir William Johnson, Colonial American, 1715–1763.* (Port Washington, NY: Kennikat Press, 1976).

Hamilton, Milton W. *Sir William Johnson and the Indians of New York.* (Albany: New York State American Revolutionary Bicentennial Commission, 1975).

Hamilton, Milton W. "Sir William Johnson's Wives," *New York History,* XXXVIII (January 1957), pp. 18-28.

Hamilton Papers. Albany Institute of History and Art, Albany, New York.

Harrison, Samuel Alexander (ed.). *Memoir of Lieut. Col. Tench Tilghman.* (Albany: J. Munsell, 1876).

Indian Castle Church Restoration and Preservation Society. *Indian Castle Church, Little Falls, New York.* (Little Falls, New York: n.d.).

Innis, Mary Quayle (ed). *Mrs. Simcoe's Diary.* (Toronto: Macmillan of Canada, 1965).

Johnson, George. Petition to Sir Peregrine Maitland, September 1, 1818. *Upper Canada Land Petitions,* National Archives of Canada, Ottawa, C2110, R.G.1, L3, Vol. 256.

Johnston, Jean. "Ancestry and Descendants of Molly Brant," *Ontario History,* LXIII, No. 2 (June 1971), pp. 87-102.

Johnston, Jean. "Molly Brant," in her *Wilderness Women: Canada's Forgotten History.* (Toronto: Peter Martin Associates Ltd., 1973), pp. 73–118.

Johnston, Jean. "Molly Brant: Mohawk Matron," *Ontario History,* LVI, No. 2 (June 1964), pp. 105-24.

Katcher, Philip R. N. *Encyclopedia of British, Provincial and German Army Units, 1775-1783.* (Harrisburg, Pennsylvania: 1973).

Kelsay, Isabel Thompson. *Joseph Brant, 1743–1807: Man of Two Worlds.* (Syracuse, New York: Syracuse University Press, 1984).

La Rochefoucault-Liancourt, François Alexandre Frederic, duc de. *Travels Through the United States of North America, the Country of the Iroquois, and Upper Canada in the Years 1795, 1796, and 1797.* (London: R. Phillips, 1799).

Lender, Mark E., and Martin, James Kirby (eds.). *Citizen Soldier, the Revolutionary War Journal of Joseph Bloomfield.* (Newark, New Jersey: New Jersey Historical Society, 1982).

Lenig, Wayne. "Archaeology, Education and the Indian Castle Church," *The Bulletin of the New York State Archaeological Association,* LXIX (March 1977), pp. 42-51.

Murray, David (ed.). *Delaware County, New York, History of the Century, 1797–1897.* (Delhi, New York: William Clark, 1898).

Namias, June. *White Captive: Gender and Ethnicity on the American Frontier.* (Chapel Hill, North Carolina: The University of North Carolina Press, 1993).

O'Callaghan, E.B. (ed.). *The Documentary History of the State of New-York.* (4 vols.; Albany: Weed, Parsons and Company, 1849-51).DHNY.

O'Callaghan, E.B., and Fernow, B. (eds.). *Documents Relative to the Colonial History of the State of New York.* (15 vols.; Albany: Weed, Parsons and Company, 1853-1887). DRCHSNY.

Ogden, John C. *Tour Through Upper and Lower Canada.* (Wilmington, Delaware: Bonsal and Niles, 1800).

Patchin, Freegift. "Story of Revolutionary Days in Schoharie County, Captivity and Sufferings of General Freegift Patchin as Related by Himself," *St. Johnsville Enterprise,* January 12-February 16, 1928. Based on interviews by Josiah Priest, c.1830.

Penrose, Maryly B. (ed.). *Indian Affairs Papers.* (Franklin Park, New Jersey: Liberty Bell Associates, 1981).

Pound, Arthur. *Johnson of the Mohawks.* (New York: The Macmillan Company, 1930).

Quinn, Kevin. "Joseph Brant: Kingston's Founding Father?", *Historic Kingston,* XXVIII (1979), pp. 73-84.

Records of St. Peter's Church, Albany, New York, 1768-1775. Photostat in New York State Library, Albany.

Reid, William D. *The Loyalists in Ontario: The Sons and Daughters of the American Loyalists of Upper Canada.* (Lambertville, New Jersey: Hunterdon House, 1973).

Reynolds, Stephen. *For All the Saints Prayers and Readings for Saints' Days According to the Calendar of the Book of Alternative Services of the Anglican Church of Canada.* (Toronto: Anglican Book Centre, 1994).

Schaaf, Gregory. *Wampum Belts & Peace Trees: George Morgan, Native American and Revolutionary Diplomacy.* (Golden, Colorado: Fulcrum Publishing Co., 1990).

Spittal, W.G. (ed.). *Iroquois Women: An Anthology.* (Oshweken, Ontario: Iroqrafts Ltd., 1990).

Stone, William L. *The Life and Times of Sir William Johnson, Bart.* (2 vols.; Albany: J. Munsell, 1865).

Sullivan, James, and Flick, Alexander C., and Hamilton, Milton W. (eds.). *The Papers of Sir William Johnson.* (14 vols.; Albany: The University of the State of New York, 1921-1965). SWJP.

Thomas, Earle. "Molly Brant," *Historic Kingston,* VII (1989), pp. 141–49.

Wilcoxen, Charlotte. "A Highborn Lady in Colonial New York," *The New-York Historical Society Quarterly,* LXIII, No. 4 (October 1979), pp. 315-45.

While no contemporary image of Molly Brant is known to exist, the possibility remains that one may reside in a collection, guarded by the owner, or simply not properly identified. The image shown here is presented as an example of the problem faced in identifying art that is not definitively documented. It is based on an engraving of a portrait which for years was purported to be of Joseph Brant and attributed to Benjamin West. The original oil-on-canvas is currently in the collection of the Yale University Art Gallery, having been gifted in 1939 by previous owner deLancey Kountze. It is known to have been sold on January 25, 1882, in the Governor Calib Lyon collection sale [George A. Leavitt & Co., New York City, lot number 85], identified as the portrait of an "Ojibbeway chief by... Benjamin West." At some point prior to 1939, Kountze, in conjunction with the Frick Art Reference Library, allowed the image to be printed and clearly identified as "Thayendonedga (Joseph Brant) by Benjamin West" [black and white image, credited to the "Avery Art and Education Fund," n.d. copy in Old Fort Niagara Archives]. However, a near exact copy hangs in the Royal College of Surgeons, London. A list of the paintings in that collection, written in 1820 by William Clift, indicates that theirs was done by William Hodges, c. 1790-91, for John Hunter. Clift stated that the portrait, and a companion piece of another American Indian, is of a Cherokee. He further notes that "These two American Indians were in London...1790-91, after the termination of the American war, and had, it appears fought on the side of the English during the struggle. I never heard their names...they were at Sir Joseph Bank's parties." This information was brought to the attention of the Yale Gallery in 1962, which heightened existing suspicions regarding the Benjamin West origin of their painting. Current cataloging at Yale (European Dept.) lists their artwork (no. 1939.40) as "British...18th century...after William Hodges (formerly attrib. to Benjamin West)....*Ojibbeway Chief*." Further noted is that "1776" is inscribed on the back. Ironically, another listing (American Dept.) contains the "Thayendonedga...West" reference, with a notation about Hodges. Further research by Yale is ongoing. Additionally, the London portrait was exhibited in Washington, D.C., identified as a "Cherokee or Creek Indian" and included in Hugh Honour's catalog *The European Vision of America* (1975; no. 185). If originated by Hodges, when stated, this could not be Brant. Was it by West after Hodges or Hodges after West? What's the origin of the Brant identification? What was the basis for the West attribution and tribe used in the Lyon sale? Is this a Cherokee, Creek, Ojibwa or other? *Sketch after West (attribution), by D.S. Knight.*

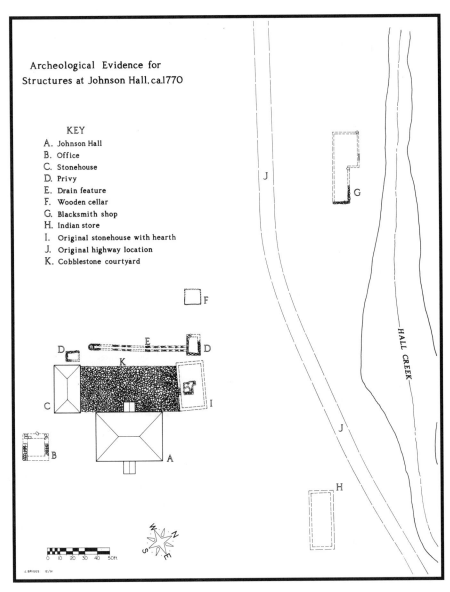

Archeological Evidence for
Structures at Johnson Hall, ca.1770

KEY

A. Johnson Hall
B. Office
C. Stonehouse
D. Privy
E. Drain feature
F. Wooden cellar
G. Blacksmith shop
H. Indian store
I. Original stonehouse with hearth
J. Original highway location
K. Cobblestone courtyard

HALL CREEK

0 10 20 30 40 50ft.

J. BRIGGS 12/91

Archaeology plan for Johnson Hall. Drawing by J. Briggs. *Courtesy, New York State Office of Parks, Recreation and Historic Preservation; Archaeology Unit, Peebles Island.*

Archaeological Remains Excavated at
JOHNSON HALL

•**Top Left: Delft Plate.**
•**Top Right : Case Bottles.**
•**Bottom Left: Interior of Punch Bowl, with words "One Bowl More" fired into the design.**
•**Bottom Right: Exterior of Punch Bowl**

All photographs courtesy, New York State Office of Parks, Recreation and Historic Preservation; Archaeology Unit, Peebles Island.

ACKNOWLEDGMENTS

Special acknowledgments go to Dr. Paul R. Huey, Scientist–Archaeologist, and Wanda E. Burch, Site Manager at Johnson Hall State Historic Site, both with the New York State Office of Parks, Recreation and Historic Preservation. They lent much help, information, and encouragement to this project. This book is dedicated to them, although the authors take full responsibility for any errors!

There are many other people and institutions to thank on both sides of the border for their support and assistance. These, in alphabetical order, are: The Albany Institute of History and Art; Robin Campbell, Curator at the New York State Office of Parks, Recreation and Historic Preservation; Kevin Decker, historian at St. George's Episcopal Church in Schenectady; Tim Donahue, photographer for the Saratoga–Capital Region, Office of Parks, Recreation and Historic Preservation; Brian Dunnigan, former Executive Director of the Old Fort Niagara Association and now Curator of Maps at the William L. Clements Library, University of Michigan, Ann Arbor; Dr. Charles L. Fisher, Kris Gibbons, Jim Gold, Cheryl Gold and Joseph McEvoy, all of the New York State Office of Parks, Recreation and Historic Preservation, Peebles Island, Waterford; George Hamell, Senior Museum Exhibits Planner in Anthropology at the New York State Museum, Albany; the Johnstown Public Library; Jim Morrison; Major Earl F. Joyner; Audrey Nieson of the New York State Office of Parks, Recreation and Historic Preservation; the New York State Library, Albany; Frank M. Packer; Jim Phillips and Daryl Carter of the Canada Post Corporation; Shelly Price–Jones; the National Archives of Canada; St. Paul's Anglican Church, Kingston, Ontario; Richard Sherman; Dr. Shirley Spragge and Lisa Russell of the Archives of the Diocese of Ontario, Kingston; William P. Stevens, historian at St. Peter's Episcopal Church, Albany; Okill Stuart, UE, of The United Empire Loyalists' Association of Canada; Sara Tyson, the artist who did the Molly Brant stamp; and Wade Wells, staff member at Johnson Hall State Historic Site.

Special thanks go out to the Old Fort Niagara Association, and its Publications Committee team: Harry M. DeBan (chairman and publisher), David J. Bertuca, R. Arthur Bowler, Craig O. Burt, III, John Burtniak, Richard Cary, Jr., William Lee Nelson-Loefke and Patricia Rice. *Molly Brant* joins their list of literary accomplishments, produced in support of the educational endeavors of the Association.

THE AUTHORS

Lois M. Huey is Scientist–Archaeology for the New York State Office of Parks, Recreation and Historic Preservation, at Peebles Island (Waterford). She received her Masters degree in Anthropology from The State University of New York at Albany, and had an undergraduate concentration in history. Huey has published articles, under the name Lois M. Feister, in *Ethnohistory* (later republished in *An Ethnohistorical Exploration of the Indians of Hudsons' River*, edited by Hauptman and Campisi), *Man in the Northeast, Journal of Field Archaeology, Historical Archaeology*, the Dutch journal *KNOB*, and other archaeology journals. She also co–authored the book *The Hudson–Mohawk Gateway: An Illustrated History*. Huey heads a team that has conducted archaeological research at Johnson Hall State Historic Site.

Bonnie Pulis is Interpretive Programs Assistant at Johnson Hall State Historic Site, Saratoga–Capital Region, New York State Office of Parks, Recreation and Historic Preservation. She received a Bachelors degree in Visual and Performing Arts from Russell Sage College, Troy, New York, majoring in Museum Theory and Practice. Pulis, along with Wanda Burch and Wade Wells, is responsible for interpretive programming at Johnson Hall, Johnstown, New York. Her responsibilities include numerous outreach programs, tours for the public and planning special events. She is co-author with Feister-Huey of the article "Molly Brant: Her Domestic and Political Roles in Eighteenth-Century New York" in *Northeastern Indian Lives, 1632-1816*, edited by Robert Grumet. (The University of Massachusetts Press, 1996).

Preserving History At Old Fort Niagara

Since 1927 the preservation and interpretation of Old Fort Niagara have been the goals of the Old Fort Niagara Association, Inc. The Association is a private, not-for-profit organization. Membership is open to anyone with an interest in the Fort and its long history. The Association operates Old Fort Niagara, a State Historic Site, in cooperation with the New York State Office of Parks, Recreation and Historic Preservation.

Old Fort Niagara Publications

Publications are an extension of the Old Fort Niagara Association's educational purpose. Created in 1984, the Publications Committee has been charged with establishing and maintaining an ongoing program of works relevant to the history of Old Fort Niagara. This includes new titles as well as the republication of older works.

• • • • • • • • •

Old Fort Niagara Association Publications Committee:

Editorial Board:
Harry M. DeBan: Chairman/Publisher
David J. Bertuca; R. Arthur Bowler; Craig O. Burt III; John Burtniak;
Richard Cary, Jr.; Mark Francis; William Lee Nelson-Loefke; Patricia Rice

Additional information about the Fort's publications, exhibits, programs, or membership in the Old Fort Niagara Association may be obtained from:

Old Fort Niagara
Fort Niagara State Park
P.O. Box 169
Youngstown, New York 14174-0169

The Molly Brant Project . . .
Production Notes
This book was produced by the Old Fort Niagara Association Publications Committee:
Harry M. DeBan, Chairman/Publisher
David J. Bertuca　　R. Arthur Bowler　　Craig O. Burt, III　　John Burtniak
Richard Cary, Jr.　　Willian Lee Nelson-Loefke　　Patricia Rice
Production Coordinator, Design & Layout: Harry M. DeBan
Editing and Research: John Burtniak, R. Arthur Bowler, Willian Lee Nelson-Loefke, Patricia Rice and Harry M. DeBan
Technical Support: David J. Bertuca, Craig O. Burt, III, and Richard Cary, Jr.
Pre-Press: Harry M. DeBan, James F. Egloff, Mark L. Bessey and Doc D.S. Knight
Production Assistance: James F. Egloff & Mark L. Bessey (Rapid Service Engraving, Buffalo, NY); Robert Emerson, Ray Wigle, Douglas DeCroix, Sue Allen, Cynthia Liddell, Dale Demler and Paul Nasca (Old Fort Niagara Staff); Brian L. Dunnigan (William L. Clements Library, University of Michigan, Ann Arbor); Matthew W. Jacobs (Digital Equipment Corporation, Syracuse, NY); Kathleen O'Malley (Hood Museum of Art, Dartmouth College); Joanna M. Weber, (Yale University Art Gallery); Harry G. & Jeannette F. DeBan, Rev. Mary Ann Nelson-Loefke, Marty Abramson, Laird A. Burkett, Keith G. Kozminski, Thomas M. O'Donnell, Michelle Sunderlin, Dean F. Ulrich and François & Sandrine du Lac.
memorare....Carl Campbell and Ted McQuilkin.